P9-EDT-286

The Story of
Daniel Boone

abridged from The Real Book About Daniel Boone

By WILLIAM CUNNINGHAM

Illustrated by Wayne Blickenstaff

SCHOLASTIC BOOK SERVICES
NEW YORK • TORONTO • LONDON • AUCKLAND • SYDNEY • TOKYO

Copyright 1952 by Franklin Watts, Inc. Abridgment copyright ©️ 1964 by Doubleday and Company, Inc. Illustrations copyright ©️ 1964 by Scholastic Magazines, Inc. This abridged edition is published by Scholastic Book Services, a division of Scholastic Magazines Inc., by arrangement with Doubleday and Company, Inc.

6th printing . . . . .February 1974

Printed in the U.S.A.

The Story of
Daniel Boone

THE DANIEL BOONE of legend is a tall, lean man in a coonskin cap who discovered Kentucky and then moved West because he did not like people.

According to this legend, he was master of the wilderness and could see a sign in "a turned leaf, a blade of grass pressed down, the uneasiness of wild animals, the flight of birds."

Like most legends, this one is only partly true. Daniel was lean, but not very tall. He never wore a coonskin cap. He was not the first white man to go into Kentucky, although he was the first to explore it thoroughly. He liked people. He moved West because he wanted to see the country.

It is true that he was master of the wilderness — one of the greatest scouts who ever lived. He was also master of himself. He did not display fright or anger. He never complained, but kept his troubles to himself.

Daniel Boone will always be remembered because he has become the symbol of the pioneer, of the adventurer who must know what lies behind the horizon. The spirit of Daniel Boone is in every boy who climbs a hill to see what is on the other side.

WILLIAM CUNNINGHAM

CONTENTS

Warriors in the Pasture

WHEN DANIEL BOONE was a boy he played Indian
with real Indians who carried tomahawks and long
rifles.

The Boones owned a piece of pasture land several
miles from their farm in eastern Pennsylvania. The
cows could not be driven all the way to the pasture
and back again every day, so Daniel's father built a
log cabin beside a spring in the pasture. Daniel and
his mother moved out there to live during the summer
months.

Daniel's job was to watch the cows and drive them
to the cabin each day at sunset for milking. But cows
do not need close watching, so Daniel was free to

wander and explore in the deep woods. This arrangement suited him just fine. He felt it was much better than working in the corn patch back at the farm.

Daniel was nine and a half — still too young to carry a gun. But he made himself a throwing spear from a hickory stick. After long practice, he became such a good spear thrower that he could sometimes kill rabbits or squirrels. To test his skill he often stalked a bear or a deer, although of course he could not kill big game with a spear made from a hickory stick.

One morning at sunrise Daniel left the cows in a glade where the grass was good. He noted carefully which way the wind was blowing, so he could easily find them again. Cows and other animals keep their faces to the wind, so they can catch the scent of things ahead of them. Daniel judged the herd would graze down toward Flying Hill.

Off in another direction a crow called. Daniel could not see the crow, but he knew it was sitting at the top of a tree as a sentry for other crows.

He decided to play that he was an Indian scout in dangerous territory, and this crow was the lookout for a band of enemy warriors. If he could creep to within shooting range of the crow without letting the crow see him, it would prove that he was a good scout. He started toward the crow.

Daniel was dressed in homespun trousers and deerskin jacket and moccasins. He was the color of the brown earth and the dead leaves. When he faded into a thicket and lay motionless, he was invisible. If he had to cross an open space, he crawled or made a swift run, bending low.

He kept his eyes constantly on the ground in front of him, looking not only for tracks but also for sluggish, fat snakes. Swift-running snakes kept out of the way. But fat, slow snakes could be dangerous. He also watched overhead for birds and noted what the squirrels were doing on high branches.

Meanwhile Daniel's ears were as busy as his eyes. They told him what was going on a hundred yards or a quarter of a mile ahead. In the deep forest, birds and small animals keep each other informed of what they see. Calm chatter and chirps and croaks mean all is well. On this day, as Daniel crept along, the crow ahead of him chatted calmly.

He could not see the crow, for he must always keep bushes and tree trunks between himself and it. But his ears told him that it was not far away, in a tree on top of a hill.

Suddenly the crow squawked and flapped into the air. Daniel froze in his tracks, thinking the crow had caught a glimpse of him. But it did not circle over him as it would have done if it had seen him. Instead it sailed about a hundred yards and settled again out of his sight. This meant the crow had seen something else, on the other side of the hill.

Squirrels on top of the hill had been chattering and rustling among the leaves on the ground. Now they raced to their trees, climbed high, and flattened themselves on branches. All at once Daniel's game became deadly serious.

Not far north, beyond a range of low mountains, were several wigwam villages of the Delaware Indian tribe. The Delawares were friendly. But far to the west lived other, unknown tribes.

Sometimes white desperados crossed the mountains into this western land and raided Indian villages, killing the Indians and taking their property. Then warriors from these wild tribes would come east to get revenge. There had been no Indian trouble in eastern Pennsylvania for a long time, but Daniel knew that such a raid was possible.

He had to get to the top of the hill to see what he could see. If he spied strange Indians, painted for war, he must race back to the cabin to warn his mother — or die in the attempt.

The best route to the top of the hill led past where the crow was calling. If Daniel went that way, the crow would see him and circle over him, cawing with new alarm, and the Indians would spot him.

There was no time to lose. Daniel crouched and ran to the top of the hill by a longer route. Only the squirrels saw him and they kept still, as he knew they would.

He crawled into a thicket and watched. In a little while he saw a movement in some bushes beside a creek. A tall Indian, carrying a long rifle, appeared.

His scalp lock stood up stiffly from his brown head. Other warriors followed, walking in single file along a deer path. They were Delawares and wore white paint, which meant they were at peace.

Daniel was greatly relieved. He was also rather pleased with himself to think that he could scout well enough to spy on Indians, even the friendly Delawares, without being seen.

There was good cover along the top of the hill, and Daniel decided to keep the Indians in sight for a while. That would be good practice. When the last warrior had passed, Daniel stood up and slipped through the bushes, ready to freeze if one of them looked back.

Suddenly right in front of him he saw a patch of tan hide, then the large, beautiful eyes of a deer. Evidently the deer had been watching the Indians, and now it was startled to discover Daniel. The deer crashed through the bushes and raced away.

One of the warriors grunted sharply and raised his rifle. The others stopped. But when they saw the deer, they decided that it alone was responsible for the commotion. They were not hunting deer, so they walked on.

For a long time, Daniel lay in the bushes, thinking. He had made a bad mistake. Looking so hard at the Indians, he had forgotten to watch the bushes right in front of him. A good scout watches everything. He decided he still had much to learn.

Daniel's Education

DANIEL BOONE was born November 2, 1734, in Oley Township, Pennsylvania, not far from where the city of Reading stands today. His father, Squire Boone, a fiery little man, was a farmer, weaver, blacksmith, and hunter. His mother was a tall, gentle woman with dark hair, who seldom scolded her many children or complained of the hardships of pioneer life. Daniel was their sixth child.

The Boone cabin stood in a clearing in the tall woods. Nearby were cabins of other pioneer families. Daniel made his first explorations in his father's blacksmith shop, in the cornfield, and in the cabins and barns of the neighbors.

He and his sister Elizabeth, two years older, watched the sparks fly when their father pounded a piece of red-hot iron. They went to the edge of the woods and played they were hunters. Or they raced to a neighbor's cabin and pretended they were wild Indians attacking a white settlement.

One summer, when Daniel was four, an epidemic of smallpox broke out. Daniel's mother informed him and Elizabeth that they must stay at home until the epidemic was over. They could not even go to the blacksmith shop, for fear they would meet someone who carried the pox on his clothes.

Daniel was very unhappy. There was nothing to do in the Boone cabin except watch his mother run a spinning wheel or his older brother operate a big clanking loom which made cloth. He complained to Elizabeth.

Elizabeth knew that once you had smallpox, you couldn't get it a second time.

"If we could catch the pox and then get better," she said, "Mother would let us go out again."

Daniel agreed that it was a good idea to catch smallpox. They did not understand that people could die from this terrible disease.

That night they crept out of the Boone cabin without a sound, ran to a neighbor's cabin, and got in bed with one of their friends who had smallpox. Then they ran back home.

A few days later they took sick. They were very

pleased about it, and their mother guessed that they were expecting this sickness.

"Daniel," she said, "I want thee to tell thy mother the truth."

The Boones were Quakers and used the old words "thee" and "thy" instead of "you" and "your."

Daniel told the truth.

His mother was distressed, but she did not become angry. She explained to him that he had done a foolish thing. Then she added, "Thee should have told me sooner, so I could be prepared."

All seven Boone children, from Sara, aged fourteen, to Mary, aged two, had smallpox. But fortunately none of them was very sick.

Probably about this time Daniel made up his mind to be a hunter rather than a farmer, weaver, or blacksmith, because a hunter does not have to stay at home.

As soon as he was old enough, Daniel trotted after his father and older brothers whenever they went deer hunting. On a day when a hunt was planned, Daniel was the first one up. Leaping from his warm bearskin bed, he shivered into buckskin trousers and rawhide boots. He splashed ice-cold water into a wooden basin and washed his face. Then he bundled himself in a bearskin coat and was ready to go.

Daniel's father realized that the boy was not cut out to be a farmer or weaver, so he began to make a hunter out of him. As soon as Daniel was big enough to aim a long rifle by resting the barrel on a stump or fallen tree trunk, his father taught him to shoot. On long trips, his father explained to him the ways of deer, bear, squirrel, and wild turkey, and told him how to load the gun for each kind of animal. Daniel learned how to tell directions in a pathless forest. He learned how to make a comfortable camp and how to kindle a fire while a freezing rain was falling.

Anything that had to do with hunting or roaming the woods Daniel learned very quickly. Other things he learned slowly or not at all.

He was good at making deerskin hunting shirts and moccasins, but awkward at operating a loom to make cloth. He liked to repair guns in the blacksmith shop, but not to sharpen plowshares. In later years he made beautiful powder horns, from cow horns, polishing and scraping them so thin that the separate grains of powder could be seen through the horn. He probably learned this art as a boy.

When Daniel was twelve years old, his father gave him a rifle, and he was the happiest boy on the frontier. The rifle was longer than he was, but by straining every muscle he could aim it without resting it on anything. When it went off, it had a powerful kick. He sometimes had to take a few steps backward to regain his balance. But after a few weeks of practice, Daniel could shoot as well as his older brothers. At stalking game he was even better than they because he was more patient and careful.

The frontier rifle of those days was over five feet long and weighed about eleven pounds. A little piece of flint rock was attached to the hammer and held in place by setscrews.

To load his rifle, Daniel carefully measured the right amount of powder and poured it into the muzzle — the front end — of the gun. Then he placed a little patch of homemade linen, with grease on it, in the muzzle. On the patch he put a round lead bullet the size of a small marble. Then he pushed the bullet and the patch down the barrel with a ramrod until the linen rested lightly on the powder. Next he put a pinch of powder in a tiny pan beneath the hammer, and he was ready to shoot.

When he pulled the trigger, the hammer came down and the flint scraped against a steel plate. Sparks flew and lighted the powder in the pan. Fire went through a tiny hole in the barrel to the powder charge. There was a bang, and a cloud of white smoke hid the target from view.

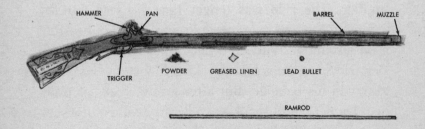

HAMMER PAN BARREL MUZZLE

TRIGGER POWDER GREASED LINEN LEAD BULLET

RAMROD

Compared with modern rifles, these guns were large and clumsy. Long practice was required to load them properly. But they were the best guns in the world at that time. And they were as accurate as modern rifles.

Daniel named his new rifle "Tick-Licker," perhaps because the hammer said "tick-lick" when it was pulled back.

From dawn until dusk Daniel was in the woods. After supper, by the light of a tallow dip, he cleaned Tick-Licker and hung it on the wall. Then he molded some bullets, refilled his powder horn, and crawled into bed, to dream of hunting and exploring.

We don't know if Daniel Boone ever went to school. Pioneer settlements in those times seldom had schools. When Daniel was fourteen or fifteen, the wife of his older brother taught him to read and write, add and divide. He liked arithmetic because surveyors used arithmetic, and Daniel thought of becoming a surveyor in the West. But he could not see any reason why a hunter and explorer should bother his head with spelling. Throughout his life he spelled by ear. A bear was always a "bar" to him, and sometimes he even spelled his name "Boon."

Daniel's father was not disturbed by Daniel's poor spelling. "Let the gals do the spelling, and Dan will do the shooting," he said.

Talk of "Bloody Ground"

By THE TIME Daniel was fifteen years old, it was hard to find a deer in the woods of eastern Pennsylvania. Daniel's father felt that there were too many people in Oley Township, and not enough game.

In the spring of 1750 Mr. Boone sold his farm and blacksmith shop. He bought covered wagons, horses, and cattle, and started southwest. His whole family went along, except for the two oldest boys, who had already married and settled down.

The Boones were in no hurry and did not know exactly where they were going. When they found good pasture, they camped for weeks and let the livestock graze. Daniel hunted to keep the family supplied with fresh meat. This was just the sort of life he liked.

For nearly two years they wandered along the eastern edge of the mountains, through western Virginia and down into North Carolina. There in the Yadkin Valley they found what they wanted — plenty of game and few hunters — so Daniel's father bought a farm on the Yadkin River. Daniel took to the woods with his Tick-Licker.

At first the hunting was too good to be any fun. Daniel could kill twenty or thirty deer in one day. But such hunting could not last long. Soon he had to wander up into the Blue Ridge Mountains to find game. Daniel knew the time would come when a man could not hunt for a living, but would have to farm. He wondered where he could go when that time came.

The friendly Catawba Indians who lived in the valley said that far to the northwest, beyond three ranges of mountains, there was a rich country called "Ken-ta-ke." It was a "dark and bloody ground," they said. The powerful Cherokee tribe lived to the south, and the fierce Shawnees to the north.

Both tribes claimed Ken-ta-ke, but neither dared to settle there for fear of the other. It was a hunting ground and a battlefield. Each summer the ground was stained with the blood of Cherokee and Shawnee warriors.

Game was so abundant there, the Catawbas said, that a man could sit beside a salt lick and kill deer, bear, and buffalo as fast as he could reload. Great herds of buffalo grazed on the plains, and their hoofs made a rumble like distant thunder. The woods were full of wild turkey.

White settlers in the Yadkin Valley also talked about "Caintuck," as they called it. But none of them had been there or planned to go. It was said that a white man would get an arrow through him before he ever set foot on the dark and bloody ground.

Some of the old hunters had heard stories that the snakes in Caintuck had stingers on the end of their tails. They rolled themselves up into hoops and chased deer. When they got up enough speed, they bounced into the air and straightened out and sailed like arrows, tail first. If they stuck their tails into any-thing — even a tree — it would swell up and burst.

Daniel did not believe everything he heard. But he wanted to see Caintuck with his own eyes. Every-thing else seemed tame by comparison. He knew that some day he would go there.

By now Daniel was almost twenty-one. He was five feet eight inches tall, with broad shoulders, thick chest, and narrow hips. He was a good wrestler, runner, and jumper. His hair was dark, and his eyes were blue beneath yellowish eyebrows. He had a slightly hooked nose, thin lips, a wide mouth, and ruddy skin. He spent most of his time alone, going on long hunts in the mountains, but he liked to be with people and attended all neighborhood gatherings.

Daniel's first big adventure occurred in 1755, shortly before his twenty-first birthday.

In 1755, France owned Canada. North Carolina and the other American colonies belonged to Britain. The French and the British were in conflict for control of the New World.

The French had built a fort, called Fort Duquesne, in western Pennsylvania, and were encouraging the Indians to attack frontier settlements. To stop these attacks, General Braddock of the British army, with a force of British soldiers and American militia, marched into the wilderness to try to capture Fort Duquesne. With Braddock was young George Washington, commanding the Virginia militia.

Also with Braddock were some North Carolina militiamen. Daniel got a job driving a supply wagon.

On the job Daniel met a most interesting man: John Finley, who had actually been to Kentucky.

Finley told Boone that Caintuck was a wonderful place. He had seen great herds of buffalo, and the woods were full of game.

"The Indians won't let you hunt there," Finley explained. "They did not mind if I went along as a trader, but they wouldn't let me kill game for myself."

"Now that you've been there and know the way, you could go without the Indians," Daniel suggested. "Let's go together when this job is over."

The job ended sooner than they expected. One day, as Braddock's forces approached Fort Duquesne, Daniel heard shots far ahead. The French and Indians were battling.

Suddenly a party of Indian warriors attacked the wagons just in front of Daniel. He had no gun. No British soldiers or militia appeared to protect the wagons. Daniel jumped on one of the horses, cut it loose, and rode for his life. The other drivers did the same.

A few months later Daniel was back in the Yadkin Valley. He did not know what had become of his friend John Finley. The trip to Kentucky now seemed an impossible dream.

Daniel might have been very unhappy at this time, except that he fell in love with Rebecca Bryan. She was the daughter of a farmer who lived near the Boones. Rebecca was rather tall, with dark hair and eyes. She was only sixteen.

They were married in August, 1756, and settled

down in a cabin on Daniel's father's farm. Less than three years later they had to flee to Culpeper County, in northern Virginia, because of Indian raids. However, in 1759 they came back to the Yadkin Valley.

For ten years Daniel lived quietly, farming in summer and hunting in fall, spring, and winter. Sometimes he ranged far. In the mountains of eastern Tennessee he cut in the bark of a tree the words, "D. Boon cilled a Bar on Tree in the year 1760." He did not guess that this tree would stand for a hundred years.

Rebecca Boone's first son, James, was born in 1757. Eight years later, Daniel started taking the boy with him on long hunts and teaching him the ways of animals who lived in the woods. When they were caught in a storm, Daniel would tuck James inside his hunting shirt to keep the boy from freezing. The hunting shirt of those days was a big, loose garment of deerskin, more like a modern overcoat than a shirt.

Daniel had not forgotten his desire to explore Kentucky. He was still saving money and making plans for such an adventure. Often he thought of his lost friend, John Finley, and the plans they had made while driving wagons behind Braddock's army.

Daniel talked about Kentucky with his neighbors and relatives. They wanted to leave North Carolina too, and find a better place to settle. Game was scarce, crops were poor, and taxes were high. They wanted to find a new frontier, where they would be prosperous and free.

Daniel's younger brother, Squire Boone, Jr., wanted to go with Daniel. Squire was a daring man, a good hunter, and almost as good a woodsman as Daniel himself. John Stuart, Daniel's brother-in-law, also wanted to go. Stuart was Boone's close friend and they often went on hunts together. The three men shared their plans and hopes.

Then one day in the early spring of 1769, when Daniel was thirty-four years old and already the father of seven children, a lean man rode up to the door of Daniel's cabin, leading several pack horses.

"Would you like to look at some nice goods just brought over from Europe?" the man inquired.

Daniel studied him a while. "Be you John Finley?" he asked.

The man's mouth dropped open with surprise. "Be you Dan Boone?"

The two had not seen or heard of each other since Braddock's defeat, fourteen years before.

The First Look

THERE MUST HAVE BEEN great excitement in the Boone cabin that night. Probably Daniel's brother Squire and his brother-in-law John Stuart were there. Daniel's sons, James, twelve, and Israel, ten, took part in the conversation and remembered it long afterward. It was a turning point in all their lives.

John Finley had gone to Kentucky again only two years before, to trade goods for pelts. The Indians had treated him well, because they profited by his trade. But they had watched him closely, so that he did not know whether he was a trader or a prisoner.

He told of a place where salt water flowed from the ground. Buffalo, deer, bear, and other animals always crowded near these salt springs. On the grassy plains were buffalo herds so large that a man might be crushed to death when they stampeded. At the falls on the Ohio River, ducks and wild geese were drawn by the current over the falls and killed. A man did not even have to shoot them. He could pick up the dead birds along the banks below the falls.

Finley knew how to get there in a boat on the Ohio River. But the Shawnees, who lived north of the Ohio, watched the river closely. If men wanted to sneak in and do some hunting, they would have to go through the mountains. Finley knew there was a wide mountain pass through the Cumberland Mountains. A trail called the "Warrior's Path" led through this "Cumberland Gap" right into the heart of Kentucky.

Daniel's two sons, James and Israel, wanted to go. They considered themselves full-grown.

Daniel shook his head. "You will have to stay and help your mother put in the crops. Some of us older men will go and see what the country is like and find some good land. Then we'll come back and get the neighbors together, so we can fight off the Indians — if they object."

On May 1, 1769, Daniel Boone, Stuart, and Finley started, with three men named Holden, Mooney, and Cooley as campkeepers. All six were mounted, and each led a pack horse carrying bearskin blankets, kettles, salt, extra guns and ammunition, and food for the trip.

They wore loose hunting shirts, trousers, leggings, and moccasins, all made of dressed deerskin. Collars of the shirts and seams of the leggings were decorated with fringes. They wore broad leather belts with the buckle in the back, so it would not catch in the brush when they crawled. A tomahawk was slung on the right side of the belt. A pouch filled with lead bullets and a powder horn were attached to a strap that passed over the right shoulder and hung down on the left side.

All the men wore coonskin caps except Daniel. He always wore a felt hat. Perhaps he felt more comfortable with a brim over his eyes.

Daniel's deerskin garments were dyed a dull black, and his long hair was braided and tied in two short "clubs" which rested on the back of his neck.

Daniel led the party through the Blue Ridge and Clinch mountains, and here they found a beaten trail toward Cumberland Gap. Indians had been taking this trail for centuries.

They traveled slowly, hunting along the way. A cold rain often drenched them, and they had to stop to dry out their deerskin garments. Daniel saw no signs that Indians had been in the mountains recently.

Near Cumberland Gap they came upon a new cabin. A man named Martin had settled there to trade with the Indians. From his cabin the trail took them to the gap, and then northwest through the hills of eastern Kentucky.

On June 7, Finley pointed excitedly at a big hill to the left of the trail.

"That's the hill I've been looking for!" he said. "Right on the other side of it are the plains I told you about. Buffalo hides! We'll be rich!"

Daniel stopped where he was. "Over there on that creek would be a good place for our main station," he said.

He was wrong, as they later learned. They built their camp too near the Warrior's Path. Indians still used this trail to cross Kentucky.

But Daniel and his men were in too much of a hurry to give the matter much thought. Daniel wanted to have a look at Kentucky. The others wanted to start accumulating a big pile of skins which would make them rich. The three campkeepers began cutting poles for the shelter. Finley and Stuart unloaded the weary pack horses.

Daniel was burning with excitement, although he was outwardly calm. Ever since he was a small boy, he had dreamed of this moment when he could see with his own eyes the rich land west of the mountains. He dismounted and started for the top of the big hill.

It was like the time years before when he watched cows in the far pasture. Only now he was really in the wilds. A few white men had been in Kentucky

before him, but they had not roamed freely. They had either hastened through along the river banks, or, like Finley, had been closely watched by the Indians.

At the top of the hill Daniel put the butt of his long rifle on the ground, rested his hands on the muzzle, and looked down. Level land as far as the eye could reach. Forest and grassy plains. It would take a year or two just to get acquainted with the rivers and forests and salt licks, and find a good place to settle.

When he returned to camp, he found that the others had built a big open-faced shelter, with walls on three sides and a steeply pitched roof of interlaced boughs. At the open side, deer meat was roasting.

No one had yet seen a fresh moccasin track or any other Indian sign. After supper the six men spread out their bearskins, lay down under the shelter with their feet toward the dying fire, and went to sleep to dream of hunting.

Dangers of the Woods

GAME WAS ABUNDANT. It would have been easy to slaughter animals close to the camp, and thus quickly build up a store of hides. But the stench of decaying flesh would have attracted flocks of buzzards. Any Indian coming within twenty miles would see the big birds and know what was going on.

The men went out in pairs on long hunts and returned at regular intervals with the hides they had taken. Daniel and Finley went together on the first long hunt, but Finley soon became ill. He was in no danger and needed only to rest a while, so Daniel went on alone to the Kentucky River. Here he saw rich land, good timber for cabin logs, and springs of pure water. He decided he would build a settlement in this place some day.

For nearly six months the men hunted and explored, and still no one saw Indian signs. When the main camp was well stocked with hides, they built outlying camps and stored the hides in them.

Along the riverbanks and near the creeks grew a stiff, bamboo-like grass called cane. The cane grew in thick clumps or "brakes," sometimes covering hundreds of acres. The stalks could grow as high as thirty feet. Buffalo wintered in the canebrakes, making trails as wide as a street.

Late in December, Daniel, John Stuart, and one of the campkeepers were living at an outlying camp near a big canebrake. One morning Daniel and Stuart went into the brake to hunt buffalo.

As they were walking along a "buffalo street," they came face to face with a party of mounted Shawnees, painted red and black for war. There was no use resisting or trying to escape.

"Pretend you're glad to see them," Boone said quickly to Stuart. "If we expect them to treat us well, they probably will." He smiled and called "How d' do," to the Indians.

A big warrior rode up to them, dismounted, and took their rifles. "How d' do," answered the warrior.

This was Daniel's first contact with the Shawnees, and he did not know their language. But he knew some of the sign language by which Indians of different tribes talked to one another. The big warrior knew a few words of English.

By signs, gestures, and words the big Indian ordered them to take him to their camp. Daniel quickly agreed.

As they approached the outlying camp, Daniel talked loudly to the Indians. The campkeeper saw them coming and ducked into the woods.

The Indians saw at a glance that it was not the main camp, because no ammunition and only a few supplies were stored there. They took the little stock of hides and ordered Daniel to lead them to the big camp.

Daniel pretended not to understand and cheerfully led them to another small camp. He wanted to give the campkeeper plenty of time to warn the men at the main camp. He was sure that the others would load their big stack of hides on the pack horses and get out of sight.

The Indians again ordered him to take them to the big camp. Again he purposely misunderstood. And when all the outlying camps had been visited, Daniel took them at last to the big one. To his dismay, the hides, the pack horses, and supplies were still there. Finley and the three campkeepers had simply hidden in the woods.

Quickly the Indians loaded the hides on the pack horses and started north, taking Daniel and Stuart with them. Evidently they did not suspect that four other white men were hiding thereabouts.

The Indians were not in a bad mood, particularly after getting all that loot. They did not want scalps of white men because they were then at peace with the whites. But their leader, a big Indian called Captain Will, made it plain that the whites had no right to hunt in Kentucky.

"What do you think they'll do with us?" Stuart asked Daniel as the two were marching along with their hands bound.

"That depends on the way we act," Daniel said. "If you think they are going to hurt you and show it, they will probably hurt you."

Going on this theory, Daniel and Stuart laughed often and pretended they did not have a worry in the world. Actually they were bitter and discouraged. They had dreamed great dreams. Now everything was being swept away.

A few days later, as they were approaching the Ohio River, Captain Will turned them loose.

"Now, brothers, go home and stay there," he said. "This is Shawnee land, and the Long Knives cannot hunt here. If you come here again, wasps and yellow jackets will sting you."

He said this not as it is written here, but by signs and gestures. Indians called white men "Long Knives," probably because white hunters carried long hunting knives.

Captain Will gave them moccasins, a short-barreled gun, and enough powder and shot to kill game for themselves on the way home. He shook hands with them and said good-bye.

Daniel and Stuart were in no mood to go home. They felt they had been robbed and insulted, and Captain Will's little joke about yellow jackets angered them. As soon as they were out of sight of the Indians, they turned and followed.

That night they crept up on the Indians, caught four horses, and rode south.

At daybreak they paused to let the horses graze. An hour later, Captain Will and his warriors rode up.

Looking into the muzzles of a half-dozen rifles, Daniel knew that his life was over if he showed the slightest fear or anger. "How d' do!" he called, in glad surprise. He laughed as if he had played a wonderful trick.

Captain Will glared at him and lowered his rifle. It is hard to shoot a man who is laughing. Captain Will dismounted. "Steal horses," he said.

He walked up to Daniel and put a bell on his neck. Then he ordered Daniel to gallop around the clearing, like a horse which has been turned out to graze. The warriors roared with laughter.

When this entertainment was over, the Indians started north again with their captives. Captain Will said he would not turn them loose this time until they were north of the Ohio River.

At dusk, when the Indians were preparing to camp for the night, Daniel and Stuart dashed into a cane-brake. The Indians took after them with whoops.

But it is very hard to find a man in a canebrake. After a long search, the Indians gave up and went to sleep.

A few days later, the two men arrived, tired and hungry, at their main camp. Finley and the three campkeepers had started home, but Daniel and Stuart soon overtook them. A gloomy conference was held beside the Warrior's Path. It was a "time of sorrow," as Daniel said later. They had lost everything except a few rifles and a little store of ammunition.

While they were talking, they heard or saw someone approaching. Daniel grabbed a rifle and stood behind a tree trunk. The others got out of sight in the bushes.

Daniel saw two men riding toward him, but he could not tell whether they were whites or Indians.

"Hello, strangers! Who are you?" he called.

"White men and friends," came the reply.

It was Daniel's younger brother, Squire, and a man named Alexander Neeley. They had brought a good supply of rifles, ammunition, traps, and other equipment.

Finley and the three campkeepers could not be persuaded to stay, and the next day they started for home. Nobody knows what became of them.

With the fresh supplies, Daniel and Squire Boone, Stuart, and Neeley established a new camp near the junction of the Red and Kentucky rivers, far from the Warrior's Path. They set traps for beaver and otter.

Each man had his own string of traps and went out alone to gather the pelts. They met at the camp every two weeks.

At one of these meetings Stuart did not appear, and Daniel went out to look for him. He found only the ashes of a campfire and Stuart's initials carved on a tree.

Stuart's disappearance frightened Neeley. For the first time he realized how dangerous it was to live in the Kentucky woods. He began to imagine brown-skinned warriors in every bush and to hear them creeping up on him at night. Finally he admitted that he could not stand it any longer. He saddled his horse and rode away.

Daniel continued to search for Stuart, but at last he gave up hope. "I loved the man like a brother," he said sadly.

Daniel and Squire Boone became more cautious. They kept together. They built a fire only at night, when the smoke could not be seen, and in a sheltered place so the flames could not be seen. Whenever possible they walked in streams, so that the current would wash away their tracks, or on hard rock or along the trunks of fallen trees. Close to camp they scattered dry leaves over their tracks. Once they saw the print of Indian moccasins near their campsite and quickly moved to another place.

By May, 1770, their ammunition was running low. Squire loaded their pelts on the horses and left for

home, promising to return late in July. Daniel remained alone, without even a horse or dog to keep him company.

He had enough ammunition to kill food for himself, but not enough to lay up a stock of hides. There was nothing to do but explore, which is exactly what he wanted to do. In later years someone asked him if he was ever lost in the wilderness. "I can't say as ever I was lost," he replied, "but I was bewildered once for three days."

While Squire was gone, Daniel went westward along the Ohio River to the falls, where Louisville is now located, and returned through central Kentucky.

One day on the return trip he discovered that Indians were following him. He tried to elude them, but there was no good cover. He ran and they took after him with whoops.

He came to the edge of a bluff and looked down. There was a sheer drop of some fifty feet and no possibility of climbing down. He was trapped.

Far beneath him was the top of a sugar-maple tree. Daniel backed off a few paces and took a running broad jump into space.

He hurtled down into the top of the tree. The limbs bent under his weight and let him gently down to the ground. He ducked into the bushes and looked up. The Indians were leaning over the edge of the cliff and talking in excited tones. It seemed to them that the white man had flown away like a bird.

Death on the Trail

DANIEL BOONE now knew more about Kentucky than any other white man. He knew its woods and plains; its streams, hills, and caves; its animals, birds, and plants.

From his experiences with Captain Will's band, he knew that the wild Shawnees living north of the Ohio River were neither monsters nor fools, but people. They would fight for Kentucky, as the whites would fight if a horde of Indians swarmed into North Carolina and took the best farms.

There was no point in hating or despising Indians just because they were Indians. That sort of hatred led to needless bloodshed. When stupid, hot-tempered white men killed friendly Indians, or killed prisoners taken in battle, or scalped fallen Indians, other whites had to suffer for it.

In all his many battles with Indians, Daniel Boone never took a scalp or permitted his men to mistreat prisoners. And he gained a reputation for honor among the Indians which often saved his life.

Squire Boone returned to Kentucky as he had promised. On July 27 the two brothers met at the appointed place. Squire reported that Daniel's wife and children were well. Squire had sold the beaver and otter pelts at a good price, and paid off his own and Daniel's debts.

With the ammunition Squire had brought, the two brothers set about the hard task of accumulating another load of hides. Sometimes they lived in caves, but usually they camped in the thick woods. Once a wolf sneaked up to their camp in the gray dawn and carried off Daniel's hat. Daniel was outraged. He had to have his hat. He trailed the wolf, shot it, and recovered his hat, somewhat chewed but still wearable.

In the fall, Squire took another load of hides east. He was supposed to return immediately, but was delayed. Daniel started east to meet him.

Soon he found Squire, and they headed for another winter of trapping. In the spring of 1771 they both started east with a valuable load of pelts. When they were almost home, they met a party of Indians who robbed them of their furs, rifles, ammunition, and horses. They reached home poorer than they had been when they began their Kentucky adventure two years before.

But Daniel did not consider the years wasted. He had learned a great deal, and he was convinced that Kentucky could be settled.

Moreover, he discovered that he was famous. From far and near, people who had heard of his exploits came to him with questions.

For two years Daniel talked about Kentucky, and people listened. Early in 1773 he and a few other men made a brief visit to Kentucky to look at the land. When they returned, Daniel heard reports that parties of settlers were preparing to move there.

Feeling there was no time to lose, Daniel sold his farm and bought horses, cattle, pigs, rifles, ammunition, and other supplies.

In September, 1773, Daniel, Squire, and about a dozen other Yadkin Valley farmers and their families — forty persons in all — started for Kentucky on horseback. They could not take wagons because the trail was so narrow at some places that a loaded pack horse could hardly squeeze through.

Probably the youngest of these pioneers was Daniel's son John, only a few months old. Rebecca must have carried him in her arms.

Daniel, Squire, and a few other men rode ahead, finding the trail and watching for signs of Indians. Women and children followed, riding gentle and dependable horses. Behind the women and children were pack horses loaded with supplies. Finally came the cattle and pigs, driven by men and half-grown boys.

There was no sign of Indians, and the frontier had been quiet for some time, so no one feared an attack. Besides, they had plenty of dogs with them. "If Indians come, the dogs will bark," they said.

In Powell's Valley, near Cumberland Gap, they passed a trading post owned by Captain William Russell. A few miles beyond the post, some of the families discovered they were running out of flour. Daniel's oldest son, James, volunteered to go back to the post and buy flour.

James was sixteen years old, and large and strong. He was a good hunter and woodsman. Daniel agreed to let him go.

James rode to Russell's post and purchased the flour. Russell's son, two white men who worked for Russell, and two Negro slaves belonging to Russell, started out with James to help him transport the flour.

When night came, they camped about three miles behind the main party.

At dawn a band of Indians fired into their camp. James Boone and the Russell boy were so badly wounded that they could not stand. One of the white workmen and one Negro were killed. The other white workman was badly wounded but ran into the woods, where he died. The other Negro was not hurt, and witnessed what followed from a hiding place in the woods.

These Indians were no better than some whites who raided Indian villages and scalped women and children. While James Boone and the Russell boy pleaded for mercy, the Indians tortured them to death.

Captain Russell, owner of the trading post, and some other men arrived at the scene of the murders soon after the Indians had departed. One of them hurried forward to warn Boone's party while the others prepared to bury the bodies.

When Daniel heard what had happened, he got his people into a ravine and posted sentries. Rebecca sent a linen sheet back to cover the body of her son. The Indians attacked the people in the ravine but were driven off. It is said that Daniel killed one of them.

While Daniel and Rebecca mourned their son, others in the group became panic-stricken. Cattle and horses had scattered through the woods, and many could not be found after the battle.

Sadly and fearfully the little party turned back. Most of them returned to their former homes in the Yadkin Valley. But Daniel and Rebecca had sold their farm and had no place to go.

There was a small fort near Cumberland Gap, called Snoddy's. Here Daniel and his family lived through the winter.

The next May, Daniel rode alone back to Powell's Valley to visit his son's grave. He found that the wolves had started digging at the graves. He dug down and made sure that the bodies had not been disturbed. Then he refilled the graves and piled logs and stones on them to keep the wolves away.

As he finished the work, a violent storm came up. The rain was so heavy that he could not see to travel.

He sat down on a log and waited while the storm howled around him. Daniel's grief for James, and the memory of many failures, brought upon him a feeling of unhappiness unlike anything he had known before. Years later he said this was the worst moment of his life.

After the storm abated, he moved some distance from the graves and lay down for the night. He could not sleep.

Suddenly he heard stealthy noises in the bushes. Indians were creeping up on him.

As quietly as possible he crawled away through the wet bushes. In the distance he heard the little bell which he had tied to his horse's neck. Slowly he made his way toward this sound, caught his horse, and mounted. He did not know how many Indians were hunting him or where they were, so he could not ride directly toward the trail.

He urged the horse forward slowly, tinkling the bell from time to time so the Indians would think the horse was still grazing. When he had ridden some distance this way, he silenced the bell and galloped off.

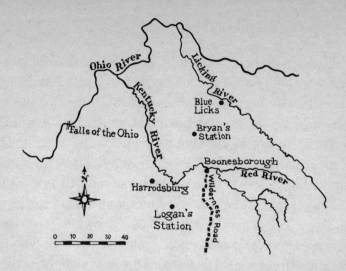

Boonesborough Is Built

THE MURDER OF JAMES BOONE and his companions in Powell's Valley was only one of many brutal acts that aroused anger on the frontier that winter. In western Virginia, a party of white men invited several Indians to their camp for a feast and killed them without reason. In North Carolina, a group of peaceful Cherokees came to a white settlement to watch a horse race. A white man stabbed one of them to death just because he hated Indians. He was not punished.

In the spring of 1774, about the time Daniel was visiting his son's grave, a man named James Harrod took thirty-four riflemen into Kentucky. They began building log cabins near the Kentucky River. The Shawnee Indians north of the Ohio heard of this and prepared for war.

The governor of Virginia knew that trouble was coming, and he sent a message to Captain William Russell, who kept the trading post in Powell's Valley. The message instructed Russell to select two "faithful woodsmen" to go to Kentucky and warn Harrod of the Shawnee danger. Russell selected Daniel Boone and a big Pennsylvania German named Mike Stoner.

Daniel and Mike made a quick trip into Kentucky and warned Harrod. Daniel had recovered from his bleak despair and was once again enthusiastic about living in Kentucky. He remained long enough in the new settlement, called Harrodsburg, to build a cabin for himself. He hoped to return soon with his family.

Daniel and Mike then turned north to warn other men who were surveying land near the Ohio River. These men thanked them and made plans to go away. Harrod and his party also departed, leaving their cabins unprotected. Daniel and Mike returned to North Carolina in August.

That fall Indians and whites were at war along the Virginia and North Carolina borders. Daniel Boone joined the militia, fought in a few skirmishes, and was promoted to captain. In October a force of militia defeated a Shawnee army on the Virginia frontier, and peace was restored. Daniel once again made plans to settle in Kentucky.

On March 10, 1775, he started for Kentucky with about thirty men, including his brother Squire, his big friend Mike Stoner, and a neighbor named Richard Callaway.

After passing through Cumberland Gap, they left the Warrior's Path and began cutting a new road toward the place on the Kentucky River which Daniel had selected long before. They called their road the Wilderness Road.

One day, as they were working on this road, one of the men called out in surprise. He found a skeleton in a hollow tree. Beside the skeleton was a powder horn with the initials J. S. Daniel saw that the powder horn belonged to John Stuart, who had disappeared on their first trip to Kentucky five years before!

One arm of the skeleton was broken and the bone still had the mark of a lead bullet on it. Evidently Stuart had been wounded by the Indians and had hidden in the tree and died from loss of blood.

On March 23 Boone's men camped in the woods some fifteen miles from their destination. At dawn the next morning they were awakened by a volley of rifle fire. There was great confusion. Some ran half naked into the woods. Two men were killed and one was wounded. At last the Indians were driven off.

Some of Boone's men were so frightened by this attack that they mounted their horses and went back to North Carolina. Daniel and the rest resumed their journey as soon as the wounded man could travel.

When they came to the Kentucky River, they saw a cheering sight — several hundred buffalo moving across a grassy plain. They would have plenty of meat in this new land.

Where Otter Creek flows into the Kentucky River, they started building a settlement which they named Boonesborough. Thirty miles to the west were the cabins which James Harrod had built the summer before. Harrod and his men were now back building more cabins.

Soon other bands of men rode into Kentucky. Some remained at Boonesborough. Others established settlements of their own.

In May, delegates from the various settlements met to establish a government for the territory, then called Transylvania. Daniel and Squire Boone and Colonel Richard Callaway represented Boonesborough.

At Boonesborough, as at other new settlements, the cabins were built around a large rectangle, facing into the center. The plan was to build a heavy log wall from one cabin to the next, to form a stockade. At a time of danger, the livestock could be kept inside the stockade. Riflemen could fire over the walls to drive off the Indians.

When a number of cabins had been built and work started on the log wall, Daniel, Squire, Colonel Callaway, and others went east to get their families.

Early in September Daniel returned with Rebecca, his son Israel, his daughter Jemima, and the four younger children. One of his daughters was already married and remained in the Yadkin Valley.

"We arrived safe," Daniel said later, "my wife and daughter being the first white women that ever stood on the banks of the Kentucky River."

There is no record of what Rebecca thought when she first saw the little line of cabins. The stockade had not been finished. If a party of Indians had attacked at that time, they could have walked right into the settlement. Winter was coming soon, food was scarce, and the supply of ammunition was running low.

Of the five hundred people who came to Kentucky that summer, three hundred lost their nerve and returned east. The troubles of Boonesborough and Harrodsburg were only beginning.

In December, a small party of Indians crept up on Boonesborough and captured two boys. Daniel Boone led a party of men in pursuit of the Indians. They found the body of one boy. No one knows what became of the other.

Meanwhile astonishing news came from the East. New England farmers and villagers had fought with British troops at Concord and Lexington, and had killed many redcoats on Bunker Hill. A man from Virginia, named George Washington, had been appointed commander of the colonial forces.

Daniel remembered this George Washington as the young soldier who had served with Braddock against the French and Indians at Fort Duquesne.

Adventure of Three Girls

Now THAT THE THIRTEEN COLONIES were in full revolt against the rule of King George, the British tried everything they could to weaken the colonial forces. They hoped to stir up Indian trouble so that General Washington would have to send part of his army West.

British agents went to the Shawnees, who lived north of Kentucky. "We will give you guns and ammunition and much war paint. The whites are taking your best hunting grounds. You can drive them out."

Probably other British agents went to the Cherokees, who lived south of Kentucky, with a similar proposition. At any rate there was much war talk among young Cherokee braves. So the Cherokees selected one of their chiefs, Hanging Maw, to go to the Shawnees and discuss the possibility of an Indian war against the whites.

Hanging Maw got his name because he had a habit of letting his big mouth hang open. But despite his funny appearance, he was a shrewd man and a good diplomat. With two other warriors he slipped into Kentucky. There he met, by accident, two Shawnee hunters, who agreed to lead him north to the Shawnee land. On the afternoon of Sunday, July 7, 1776, the five Indians crept into a canebrake across the river from Boonesborough. That same afternoon Daniel Boone was resting in his cabin. Because he had been to meeting that morning, he was not dressed in his usual buckskin garments, but wore his best trousers, made of homespun cloth.

He took off his coat and hung it on a peg, removed his shoes and shoved them under the bed, where the children would not stumble over them. He pulled off his stockings and stretched out for a nap.

His daughter Jemima, now fourteen, was visiting at the Callaway cabin with her friends Betsey, sixteen, and Fanny, fourteen. All three girls wore their Sunday-go-to-meeting dresses, with long skirts which came to their ankles. Betsey wore shoes. Grown women of Boonesborough wore shoes only on Sunday. Jemima Boone and Fanny Callaway still did not have Sunday shoes, and so were barefoot.

Betsey Callaway wanted to go for a walk, but Jemima had stepped on a cane stub that morning and hurt her heel.

"Let's go for a canoe ride," Jemima said. Fanny

also voted for a canoe ride. So the three went down to the riverbank, climbed into Daniel's birchbark canoe, and shoved off.

They had much to talk about — namely, three boys. Betsey was soon to be married to handsome Samuel Henderson. Fanny had her eye on John Holder. Jemima Boone was in love with Flanders Callaway, a cousin of Betsey and Fanny's. But Jemima was unhappy because her father considered Flanders a green youth. He said that Flanders and Jemima were too young to get married.

The three girls talked for a long time until they noticed that the current had carried them far down the stream and close to the opposite shore, near a canebrake.

It was just at this spot that Hanging Maw and his four companions had hidden in order to spy on Boonesborough.

A brown arm reached out and grabbed the canoe. The girls screamed, but they were too far from the settlement to be heard. Fanny struck one warrior with her paddle so hard that the paddle broke, but he was not hurt at all. He grabbed Betsey by the hair and flourished his knife. This meant that he would scalp her if she did not keep quiet. The girls quit screaming.

The braves lifted them from the boat and carried them across a hill, out of sight of the river. Hanging Maw knew some English. "Your name?" he asked Jemima.

"Jemima Boone," she said proudly.

"Boone!" Hanging Maw exclaimed. Every Cherokee knew of the great hunter, Daniel Boone.

"Your sisters?" he asked, pointing to the Callaway girls.

"Yes," Jemima lied. She believed the other girls would get better treatment if the Indians thought they were also daughters of Daniel Boone.

Jemima knew a great deal about Indian ways from what her father and others had told her. She guessed that these warriors did not intend to kill them, but would take them away as captives. Their only hope was to delay the Indians as much as possible and leave a plain trail for Boonesborough men to follow.

Her foot suddenly became so "sore" that she could hardly step on it. She stopped and complained. An Indian shoved her and she fell down, probably digging her fingers into the earth, so her father would see these handprints. Now Fanny's feet also became "tender."

Beneath his war paint, Hanging Maw had a kind heart. He dug into a supply pack and took out two pairs of moccasins, the smallest he could find, and gave them to the barefoot girls. With his scalping knife he cut the girls' skirts off at the knees so they could walk more easily. Then he helped them bind the cloth around their bare legs as protection against brambles.

After this considerable delay, the little party started north. Jemima stumbled, clutched a bush, and fell down. She had broken a little branch on that bush. In a short time the leaves of the broken branch would begin to wither, and Daniel Boone would know they had passed this way.

While the Indians were watching Jemima, Betsey dropped a corner of her handkerchief on which the name Callaway was embroidered.

After covering some ten or twelve miles, the Indians camped for the night. They gave the girls smoked Buffalo tongue for supper. This was a great delicacy on the frontier.

At daybreak the march began again, and soon they came upon a stray pony in the woods. Hanging Maw caught the pony and put the girls on it.

There was a scream. Jemima fell off.

Patiently he put Jemima back. She fell off again, dragging the other girls with her.

Now Hanging Maw himself mounted the pony and showed them how to ride. It was no use. Finally, the Indians decided that white squaws just could not learn to ride, so they turned the pony loose and forced the girls to walk.

Meanwhile there was great excitement at Boonesborough. Before Daniel finished his Sunday nap, someone saw the empty canoe on the other shore and shouted the alarm. Daniel leaped up, grabbed his rifle, and ran out barefoot. Young Samuel Henderson, who was engaged to marry Betsey, was shaving when the alarm came. He rushed out with half his face unshaven.

Daniel and the other men crossed the river and

soon found the trail. They easily guessed what had happened. Daniel said they must follow afoot and try to take the Indians by surprise.

He started out, studying the ground, and the others followed. They were all dressed in their Sunday clothes, which were not suitable for a job like this.

When night came and they could no longer see the trail, they lay down to rest. One man went back to Boonesborough and returned with a pack of buckskin clothes, moccasins, ammunition, and jerked venison.

At dawn they started again, finding broken branches, heel prints, and bits of handkerchief. Perhaps the Indians wanted to be followed. Daniel told his men to watch for an ambush.

Daniel led his men along the trail until the middle of the afternoon. Then he stopped. The trail ended abruptly at a stream.

The men examined every inch of ground on a dozen buffalo streets leading from the canebrake on the bank of the stream. But they found nothing.

Already the Indians were far ahead. There seemed no hope of overtaking them before they reached the Ohio River. If the girls were taken across the Ohio, not even an army could rescue them.

Suddenly Daniel called to the men. "Never mind the trail," he said. "They don't want us to follow any farther. That means they're not planning an ambush. They're heading for the Shawnee camps on the Scioto

River. I know how they'll go."

He set off at such a rapid pace that only the most athletic of the men could keep up.

Once he turned to Flanders Callaway, Jemima's friend, who was right at his heels, and said, "You're coming along just fine." Flanders was greatly pleased.

At night the men flung themselves down for a few hours of sleep, and at dawn they started again. Daniel stopped on the bank of a small stream. "They crossed hereabouts," he said. "Look for tracks."

They followed the stream and, within two hundred yards, they found fresh tracks. The water was still muddy.

An hour later they found the carcass of a buffalo which had been killed that morning.

"At the next watering place they'll stop to cook the meat they cut from this carcass," Daniel said.

Now the men crept forward with great caution. One of them found a snake which the Indians had killed. It was still wriggling. About noon they came to the next watering place.

Meanwhile the three girls were waiting for dinner in a clump of trees on the other side of the stream. They had no idea that help was near. They were now more than thirty miles from Boonesborough.

One of their captors had been posted as a sentry on a hill. Another built a fire. A third Indian lazily put buffalo meat on a stick for roasting. Hanging Maw went down to the stream to fill a kettle.

The sentry was so sure that no whites were about that he leaned his rifle against a tree and came down to the fire to light his pipe.

Jemima was watching the Indian put meat on the stick, when suddenly a spurt of blood seemed to come from the brown skin on his shoulder. A shot rang out.

The wounded Indian fell into the fire but leaped up and sprinted for a canebrake nearby. Betsey Callaway started to run. The sentry hurled a tomahawk past her head.

"Fall down!" came a command.

The girls recognized Daniel's voice and fell to the ground. Guns blazed everywhere.

In their disorderly retreat to the canebrake, none of the Indians had time to grab up a rifle, so the whites did not fear an attack. They sat down and ate the meat which the Indians had left.

Next morning the party started home. On the way they caught the stray pony, and now the girls could ride very well!

As soon as they reached Boonesborough, Samuel Henderson finished shaving. Within a month he and Betsey were married. There was "dancing to fiddle music by the light of tallow dips, and a treat of homegrown watermelons of which the whole station was proud."

Daniel and Jemima had a private talk. "I was wrong about Flanders Callaway," Daniel admitted. "He's a real man."

When Jemima married Flanders and Fanny married John Holder, the watermelon season was past, but there was again much dancing to fiddle music.

There was one other great celebration that year. A traveler arrived with a newspaper only a few months old. The Boonesborough citizens gathered, and someone read aloud the Declaration of Independence. The thirteen colonies, and Kentucky, were now free and independent.

The settlers built a bonfire. The fiddlers tuned up, and there was more dancing. Never again would the British king tell them what to do.

History tells us that Hanging Maw got back to the Cherokee country safely. He lived to a ripe old age, finally becoming a good friend of the whites.

Blood Freezes on a Blade

On New Year's Day, 1777, a little procession of exhausted men and women and frightened children halted at Boonesborough. They were fleeing from McClelland's Station, farther north. For two days they had defended their stockade against a strong force of Indians, but they knew they could not withstand another such attack. They were going east to safety.

Ten Boonesborough men went with them. They too had seen too much of the dark and bloody ground. Only thirty riflemen now remained at Boonesborough.

From Harrodsburg came word that Indians had killed two men. Other settlements reported that several of their hunters had been killed near the Licking River. Worry grew into panic. Most of the newer settlements were abandoned, leaving only Boonesborough, Harrodsburg, and Logan's Station still occupied. Logan's was about twenty miles south of Harrodsburg.

At Boonesborough, the settlers worked night and day to strengthen the walls of the stockade and lay in enough supplies to withstand a siege. Only the most skillful hunters and woodsmen were permitted to go out for game. Others went out in large groups to gather wood, and they kept their rifles handy.

A tall, lean man named Simon Kenton, about twenty years old, went into the woods alone each day to watch for Indians. Simon was an excellent woodsman, well able to take care of himself. If an Indian army had approached, Simon would have given the settlers at least a few hours' warning. But he could not scout every ravine for little bands of warriors.

On the morning of April 14, Simon helped a boy open one of the heavy gates of the stockade to let the cows out. But Squire Boone's old cow Spot did not want to go out.

"That cow smells Injuns," Simon said.

Two settlers walked past. "What does a cow know about Injuns?" they said. They went out into the clearing.

Suddenly Simon and the boy heard a shout. One of the men who had just left was racing toward them. An Indian was scalping the other, not sixty yards from the gate.

Simon raised his long rifle and fired. The Indian fell dead.

Simon calmly reloaded. As he did so, two other Indians leaped from the bushes to pick up the body of their fallen comrade.

Daniel Boone and others heard the shot and rushed out with rifles ready. Despite his long experience in Indian warfare, Daniel made a mistake. He ran toward the Indians. A dozen men, including Simon, followed him.

When they were about a hundred yards from the stockade, they heard war whoops behind them. A party of warriors had dashed in from the side and cut them off from the stockade.

"Back to the gate!" Daniel ordered. "Charge them!"

Rifles crashed, and the air was filled with white smoke. There was no time to reload. Whites fought with rifle butts, and Indians with tomahawks.

Simon Kenton was not one to waste powder. He held his fire until the smoke cleared away. Then he saw that Daniel was down and an Indian was running toward him with a scalping knife. Simon fired and the Indian fell.

Another Indian leaped at Daniel. Simon knocked him down with the rifle butt, thus saving Daniel's life twice in a couple of minutes.

The big Pennsylvania German, Mike Stoner, was in the thick of the fight when a bullet hit his arm. He fell.

Another big man ran to help him up.

"Get away from me altogether," Mike roared. "We make too big a lump to shoot at." He got to his feet and staggered toward the fort.

The Indians ran for cover, carrying their dead and wounded. Simon picked up Daniel and carried him toward the stockade.

As soon as they could reload, the Indians opened fire from the bushes and canebrake. Bullets whistled past Simon's ears and kicked up dirt in front of him. Jemima Callaway, Daniel's daughter, ran from the stockade and helped Simon carry Daniel to safety.

Boonesborough was lucky that day. Only the man who was scalped before the shooting was dead. Daniel had a broken ankle and Mike Stoner a broken arm.

On July 4, before Daniel's ankle healed, a large force of Shawnee warriors surrounded Boonesborough. For two days bullets slapped against the logs of the stockade, and flaming arrows struck cabin roofs. Inside the stockade, men fired through loopholes, while women and children beat out the flames. Then the Indians stole away.

Daniel knew that this was only a sample of what was to come. The Shawnees were testing the strength of the Kentucky whites.

Soon after, about two hundred white riflemen arrived from Virginia and North Carolina, but only fifty of them remained at Boonesborough. The others went to reinforce the garrisons at Harrodsburg and Logan's Station.

By January, 1778, all three Kentucky settlements were out of salt, which was used not only for seasoning but also for curing meat and hides. About thirty men from the three settlements went to Blue Licks and began the tedious work of making salt.

They filled big iron kettles with salty water from a spring and boiled off the water. About eight hundred gallons of water yielded a bushel of salt. A bushel of salt was worth as much as a cow, so their work was profitable.

Blue Licks was far north of Boonesborough and only about a day's march from the Ohio River. It was right on the trail from the Shawnee country to the Kentucky settlements. But the men felt fairly safe because they did not expect a large Indian army to enter Kentucky in the middle of the winter. For nearly a month all went well.

One day early in February, Daniel Boone, hunting alone, killed a buffalo in a canebrake some five miles from the salt camp. He butchered the buffalo and tied a heavy load of meat on the back of his saddle horse.

Snow was flying and the wind was very cold. Daniel's hands were numb, and he was in a hurry to get back to camp. Carelessly he thrust his long knife into its sheath without wiping the blood from the blade.

He was leading his horse along a narrow trail, past the upturned roots of a fallen tree, when the horse startled. Daniel looked back and saw the barrel of a long rifle moving in the bushes.

He grabbed his knife, planning to dump the meat and gallop away on the horse. But the blood on the knife blade had frozen, and he could not pull it from

the sheath. He dropped the reins and ran.

A rifle crashed and a bullet whined past him. Four Shawnee braves were sprinting after him with war whoops. There was no good cover and his tracks were plain in the snow, so he could not hide. When the braves reached his horse, one of them cut the thongs, dumped the load, and mounted. Daniel could not outrun the horse.

Two more shots rang out. Daniel discovered that a bullet had cut the strap which held his powder horn and the horn had fallen into the snow. He could fire only one shot.

He knew escape was impossible. He stopped, leaned his rifle against a tree as a sign of surrender, and waved at the Indians.

As the warriors came panting up to him, he remembered his old rule that people treat you pretty much as you expect to be treated. "How d' do," he said, smiling.

The braves took his rifle and tried to yank his knife from the sheath. He helped them pry it loose. Then they said "How d' do" and shook hands.

This was like old times, when Captain Will had captured Boone and Stuart, and scolded them for hunting. He hoped these Indians would merely march him north for a few days and turn him loose.

But such hopes vanished an hour later when the braves led him to campfire some thirty feet long. Around it sat more than a hundred Shawnees in war paint, and a few white men.

One of the braves who had captured Boone made a lengthy speech in a high, singsong voice. Boone understood only the words "Boone, big chief of the Long Knives." The rest of the speech probably emphasized the bravery of the speaker and his companions, and told how cunning they were to capture Boone.

Daniel hoped that the speaker also mentioned that the leader of the Long Knives showed no fear upon being captured. At that moment Daniel's life depended upon the impression he made. He must be calm, somewhat amused, careless of his own fate. But not careless enough to provoke some young hothead into striking him with a tomahawk.

During the speech, the braves sat motionless. Some spat into the fire, indicating their contempt of the white chief. When the speech was finished, several older men arose, said "How d' do," and shook hands.

Boone knew this was no gesture of friendship, but merely a salute, recognizing Boone's rank. Indians sometimes shook hands with a respected captive before putting him to death.

Daniel recognized one of the braves. "Captain Will!" he exclaimed.

Captain Will stared at him with no sign of recognition.

With gestures and the few Shawnee words he knew, Boone reminded Captain Will of their previous meeting.

"You steal my horses," he said. "I steal them back.

You steal them again. You put bell on my neck. I run away. You can't find me." He haw-hawed. This was a good opportunity to prove that he was not afraid to taunt his captors.

Captain Will remembered now. He laughed, and shook hands again. This was a good omen.

One dark-skinned brave spoke to Boone in good English. His name was Pompey. He was a Negro who had been a slave of the whites, but had escaped and joined the Shawnees.

"Chief Blackfish wants to talk to you," Pompey said.

He led Boone to a short, powerfully built man with fierce, deep-set eyes. An old record tells of their conversation. "Who are the men at the salt springs?" Blackfish asked.

Daniel hesitated. This was a blow. He had hoped the Indians did not know of the others.

"They are my men," he said finally.

"Good! Tomorrow morning we will surround their camp and kill them."

Daniel Thinks Fast

"**Y**OU COME TO KILL MY PEOPLE because the British paid you," Daniel Boone said to Chief Blackfish.

The chief did not change expression. He spoke slowly.

"That is not true. When the redcoats came to us with offers, we refused. Our great Chief Cornstalk went to the fort of the Long Knives on Mount Pleasant on the Ohio River to talk peace. But the Long Knives murdered him and his son, although they came in peace, without guns. The spirit of Chief Cornstalk calls out from the grave for us to avenge his murder."

Daniel knew that the Indians could surround the salt camp and take the men by surprise. It was unlikely that any one of them would escape to warn Boonesborough. The people of Boonesborough would not be expecting an attack in the dead of the winter. The stockade still needed repairs. A war party this size could capture the fort.

When Boone answered Blackfish, he spoke with great care.

He explained that the Long Knives who murdered Chief Cornstalk were not from Kentucky, but belonged to another tribe.

"The Long Knives in Kentucky," he added, "are tired of fighting the Shawnees. They cannot hunt or grow corn while the fighting goes on." He suggested that the Boonesborough Long Knives, with their women and children, might be willing to go north and live with the Shawnees. But they could not go peaceably in winter. They would rather fight a battle than travel with their women and children in cold weather. Next summer would be different, he hinted.

Finally Daniel suggested that he himself would go to the salt camp and tell his men to surrender peacefully, if the Indians would promise to treat them well and not make them run the gantlet. Daniel said the men at the salt camp would go north now with Blackfish. Next summer he himself would lead Blackfish's men back to Boonesborough and tell all the others there to surrender.

Blackfish talked it over with the other chiefs. Then he told Daniel that the men at the salt camp would not have to run the gantlet if they surrendered without firing a shot.

The next morning Boone walked into the salt camp. Some fifty steps behind him came three Indians, with rifles pointed at his back. The men of the camp seized their rifles, but Daniel called to them that they were surrounded and resistance was useless.

The men stacked their arms. The Indians came in from all sides and bound their hands behind them. Daniel was relieved to see that Flanders Callaway was not there. He would carry the word to Boonesborough.

Then the Indians sat down for a council of war. Pompey, sitting next to Daniel, translated for him.

A young brave arose and said that Long Knives had invited Chief Cornstalk in for a talk and then murdered him. Chief Cornstalk's spirit cried for revenge. Now the Shawnees had thirty Long Knives who should be roasted to death, one at a time.

Daniel looked quickly at Blackfish. The old chief had his usual stern expression, but Daniel could see no sign of surprise or anger on the copper features.

Daniel knew that an Indian chief was not an absolute ruler of his people, but was regarded as a father or older brother. In the heat of battle, he commanded; at other times he only advised. If the majority of the warriors wanted to kill their prisoners, Blackfish would be helpless to protect them.

Daniel had about the same degree of authority over his own men. They usually followed his advice, but they felt no compulsion to do so.

Another brave arose. The Long Knives, he said, were no good. They crept up on villages and killed women and children. They could fight only when they were hiding behind a fence of big logs. Long Knives were cowards, and should be killed without all this argument.

An older chief arose now and spoke calmly. He agreed that white men had done bad things. He agreed that they were cowardly and weak. But on the other hand the Shawnees must be wise. They would have great glory when they got home. The British would pay much money for these captives. The Shawnees should take these men to the redcoats at Detroit.

A white man stood up next. He was a Frenchman, but was acting as a British agent. He could speak Shawnee. He said it made no difference whether the Shawnees killed these captives or not, but they should go immediately to attack Boonesborough.

Finally, after many had spoken, Blackfish signaled to Boone that he was to speak. Daniel stood up.

"Brothers," he said, as Pompey translated into Shawnee, "What I have promised you I can much better fulfill in the spring than now. Then the weather will be warm, and the women and children can travel."

Boone told the Shawnees that if they killed his men, the Great Spirit would be displeased, and the Shawnees would not have success in hunting or war.

He told the Shawnees that his men would make good warriors and hunters if they were permitted to live and to join the Shawnees.

"They have done you no harm, and they surrendered as I advised them. Spare them, and the Great Spirit will smile upon you." He sat down.

Then the matter was put to a vote. A war club was passed around. If a warrior struck the ground with it, he was voting to kill the whites. Fifty-nine struck the ground. Sixty-one did not.

The young warriors glared at Daniel. He knew that if he or the other captives did anything to anger the warriors, another vote would be taken, with different results.

The Indians now unbound their captives and put them to work loading plunder on the horses. Blackfish stood with arms folded. Ordinarily when work was to be done, Daniel worked harder than anyone else. But he decided he must now play the part of chief. He folded his arms.

After the horses were loaded, a fierce-looking young Shawnee handed Boone a brass kettle and said something in contemptuous tones.

"He says you are to carry this kettle on the march," Pompey explained.

"I am to carry a kettle?" Daniel laughed and threw the kettle down into the snow.

The young brave leaped at him with a roar.

Daniel swung and connected solidly with the brave's chin. The brave's feet flew up, and he landed on the back of his neck in the snowbank.

There was complete silence. Everyone stood staring. The fallen brave sat up with a dazed look on his face and rubbed his chin.

Then an old chief whooped with laugher. The other Shawnees joined. The forest rang with their mirth. The brave got to his feet, and then he too laughed.

After this, the young braves eyed Boone with wonder. They had always taken it for granted that white men were weaklings and cowards. But if the white chief could knock a Shawnee flat on his back, it proved that there was some good in the white race.

They marched north. Daniel's men were all strong and healthy, so they could keep up the pace. Toward evening the column halted, and the Indians gave the captives a good supper. But when the meal was over, Daniel noticed that the Indians were clearing a wide path in the snow and arming themselves with heavy sticks, deer antlers, and other blunt weapons. He knew what this meant: the gantlet.

"Tell Chief Blackfish," he said to Pompey, "that he promised my men would not have to run the gantlet."

"Chief Blackfish," Pompey said, "remembers his promise and will keep it. The gantlet is for you. He did not promise that you would not have to run."

Daniel admitted that he had forgotten to mention himself.

"Tell your chief," he said, "that he is an honorable man, and I am glad that I can run the gantlet. Before I join the Shawnees, I want to know whether they are weak like children or are strong men who can hit hard."

The Indians formed two rows facing each other. Daniel took his place, lowered his head, and charged between the two lines of men. As he entered the gantlet he zigzagged, so that he was too far from one man and too close to another to get the full force of their blows. Then he stopped, leaped forward, dodged.

One brave stepped in front of Boone to get in a good blow, but Daniel butted him in the chest and knocked him over backward. Again the woods rang with Shawnee laughter.

It took a long time to get through the line this way, but Daniel probably got fewer solid blows than he would have if he had sprinted.

When it was over, the Shawnees helped him bind his bloody head and shook hands with him, this time in real friendship.

For ten days they trudged in bitter cold. Some of the Indians suffered from frozen ears, but they did not complain. Not accustomed to or properly dressed for long marches in winter weather, the Indians had a worse time than the whites.

About half of the captives imitated Daniel, marching along stolidly, pretending they were neither tired nor cold. The others complained and snarled at one another and at the Indians.

One man, Andrew Johnson, played a game of his own. He was a tiny fellow, and looked like a young boy. When he was given a load, he fell down and cried. He was such a pathetic creature that the Indians took pity on him and let him stagger along without carrying anything. Daniel was greatly amused by this, because he knew that Andrew was strong as an ox.

After they crossed the Ohio River, game was scarce, and often there was nothing to eat except the bark of white oak and slippery elm. The Indians divided the food equally and were just as hungry as their captives.

On the eleventh day they stopped, and the Indians began painting their faces and fixing themselves up. Pompey explained that they were near the great Shawnee town of Chillicothe and were preparing for a grand march into town.

Dozens of Indian women came from the town and picked up most of the booty, so the braves could march in without burdens. The white captives were given big loads. Those captives who had complained during the march were stripped naked and given extra loads. Daniel and little Andrew Johnson did not have to carry anything.

The town consisted of several hundred wigwams and a big council house. Singing and whooping, the warriors marched into town and did a war dance. It was plainly a great occasion.

When the war dance was over, the warriors took their captives into the council house. Here the naked ones were permitted to put on their clothes. There was a long powwow with speeches and arguments. Late in the afternoon the session was adjourned for a feast. The captives were not invited to the feast, but were well fed.

The next day the powwow was resumed. Votes were taken, and Boone was voted a fine fellow. Blackfish himself announced that he intended to adopt Boone as a son. Other warriors asked to adopt whites who had behaved well on the trip. The complaining whites were voted "no-good." They were to be sold to the British at Detroit.

The "no-goods" were happy. They had been smart to complain, even though they had to march into town naked. It was much safer to be a prisoner of the British than of the Indians.

Little Andrew Johnson was a special problem. It seemed unlikely that the British would pay anything for a foolish child. But one old chief said that he and his wife wanted to adopt Andrew. They had lost a son and were lonesome. They said they would treat Andrew well, and maybe he would grow up to be a warrior.

Blackfish then announced that he and forty warriors would take the "no-goods" to Detroit for sale. He would also take Daniel Boone along, as a sort of prize exhibit to impress the British. He would, of course, bring Daniel back.

Daniel Becomes
Big Turtle

THE OLD CHIEF who adopted Andrew began training him almost immediately. He put a light load in a rifle, showed Andrew how to aim, and asked him to shoot at a tree. Little Andrew raised the heavy gun, closed his eyes, and pulled the trigger. The gun kicked him over backward. The Indians laughed.

" 'Pequolly,' " they said, which meant "Little shut-his-eyes." From then on, Andrew's name was Pequolly.

The Indian children liked to tease him. "Pequolly," they would ask, "which way Kentucky?"

Pequolly would look up at the sky, think a while, and point in the wrong direction. The old chief and his wife were sad. Their adopted son, it seemed, was not only afraid but weak-minded.

One morning Pequolly was gone. The old chief could not find his best rifle, powder horn, and bullet pouch. He was in despair.

"I scolded Pequolly," he said, "and that's why he ran away. He will die in the woods, and wolves will eat him."

Searching parties were sent in all directions, for there was no telling which way Pequolly would wander. They could find no trace of him. After several days, when they felt sure he was dead, they gave up the search.

A few weeks later, a little party of Shawnee hunters who had camped near Chillicothe were awakened at dawn by rifle fire.

"Hey," they called, "we are Shawnees!" They supposed that another Shawnee party had mistaken them for enemies.

The rifle fire continued. Bullets kicked up ashes of the campfire and cut twigs from bushes. They crawled to safety, very much puzzled. When the shooting stopped, they looked around and found that their seven pack horses were gone.

Returning to Chillicothe, they told their story in the council house. The chiefs wondered what tribe would have the courage to send a party into the heart of Shawnee territory to steal horses.

A few days later the mystery was solved. A lone hunter arrived and said he had seen Pequolly and five other whites take seven horses across the Ohio into Kentucky.

Now the old resentment against the whites flared up again. Young braves made speeches. White men, they said, are weak and timid, but full of beastly cunning. Pequolly is no child, but a dangerous man. He found his way back to Kentucky and now is leading raiding parties into the Shawnee land.

The old men admitted they had been fooled by Pequolly, but they said the wrong magic had been used when Pequolly was adopted.

"The white blood was not all washed out of him, and so he betrayed us."

When Blackfish and Boone returned to Chillicothe from Detroit, they found a bad situation. The young braves wanted to kill their white captives and march immediately into Kentucky to destroy the white settlements.

But the older Shawnees did not want war if it could be avoided. They had seen too much of war.

In order to keep his position as chief, Blackfish had to please both sides. He proposed that the Shawnees continue to treat their captives well and adopt them into the tribe. Then when warm weather came, the Shawnees would raise a large army and march into Kentucky. If the whites surrendered, as Boone had promised, no lives would be lost. If they did not surrender, the Shawnees would destroy them.

The young braves did not like this compromise, but they agreed to it.

Blackfish made a big ceremony of Daniel's adoption into the tribe. One afternoon an old Indian came to see Daniel in Blackfish's wigwam, bringing a piece of bark with a little pile of ashes on it.

Daniel sat down. The old man dipped his fingers in the ashes, took hold of a lock of Daniel's hair, and yanked it out. The ashes on his fingers helped him get a firm grip. Though the pain was intense, Daniel did not wince. The hair-pulling continued until only a scalp lock was left on top of Daniel's head. Then the old man braided a string of beads and silver ornaments into Daniel's scalp lock.

Daniel then took off his clothes and put on a breech-cloth, so the old man could paint his face and body with the colors and patterns of the tribe. Finally Daniel put on silver bracelets and armbands and other ornaments.

Blackfish led him outside and summoned the Indians. People came running from all wigwams. While Daniel shivered in the raw spring wind, Blackfish made a speech, explaining that Boone was to become his son.

After that, the most prominent old women of the town took Daniel down to the river and scrubbed him from head to foot to "wash out the white blood." He was handed a staff and instructed to march to the council house.

Here a pile of presents awaited him, including

hunting clothes, blankets, a ruffled shirt, leggings decorated with ribbons and beads, and a pair of moccasins. He put on some of this finery. His face was again painted, and red feathers were tied in his scalp lock. He was given a pipe and tobacco and a tomahawk.

Now all the warriors of the town marched in, dressed in their best garments. Everyone sat down on the benches lining the wall. Pipes were lighted, and the warriors sat for a time in silence. Daniel lighted his pipe and took a few puffs, for ceremonial reasons. He did not enjoy the pipe because he was not a tobacco user.

Finally Blackfish made a speech. Daniel could now understand Shawnee fairly well and did not need a translator.

Blackfish said that every drop of white blood had been washed out of Daniel.

"You are taken into the Shawnee nation and initiated into a warlike tribe," he said. "You are adopted into a great family. We are now under the same obligation to love, support, and defend you as we are to love and defend one another. My son, you have nothing to fear."

Daniel was given the name of Sheltowee, which meant "Big Turtle," and was personally introduced to each warrior.

Boone was now officially a Shawnee, but he was not easy in his mind. Most of the young men still considered him white and hated him for that reason. Even the old chiefs looked upon him with suspicion. Daniel knew that any warrior would shoot him if he tried to run away. Yet he knew he would have to escape soon to warn the settlers at Boonesborough.

Old Blackfish treated his new son with every kindness, but he was shrewd enough to know what was in Daniel's mind. Blackfish kept careful count of the bullets he gave Daniel. Whenever Daniel returned from a hunt, Blackfish asked how many shots he had fired and what he had killed. Generally Daniel had to tell the truth, because he knew Indian scouts had watched him. However, he devised ways to deceive his watchers.

Sometimes, while gazing into a tree pretending to look for squirrels, he cut a bullet in two. With a half-bullet he could kill a squirrel or turkey. Of course, he had to be careful not to bring home a turkey with a half-bullet lodged in its body.

Often he pretended to be eating a piece of jerked venison, while actually he stuffed the meat into the sleeve of his hunting shirt. In this way he slowly accumulated a little store of food and bullets, which he kept hidden in a leather sack under his shirt.

One day on a hunt, while sharp eyes were watching from a distance, he sat down beside a tree and gazed upward for a long time. His hands, out of the sight of the watchers, were very busy digging a hole and burying the sack.

On days that Daniel did not hunt, he busied himself about the town. Remembering the skill he had learned in his father's blacksmith shop, he repaired rifles for the Indians. Even without a forge and anvil, he could sometimes fix a gun which the Indians considered beyond repair.

Once they brought him a rifle without a stock. He shook his head over this job, saying it would take a long time to fix. He laid the rifle aside until the Indians had forgotten all about it. Then he hid it in the woods.

A Race for Life

Boone now spoke Shawnee so well that he could always make himself understood. However, children often laughed happily at the way he talked. He joined in their fun, and deliberately made mistakes to keep people in good humor.

Some of the children became Daniel's special friends. He traded various trinkets he had for maple syrup or sugar, and he gave these sweets to his young friends. Imitating his speech, they called it "molass'."

The Shawnees did not live an easy life. Sometimes there was nothing at all to eat, and the people grew weak from hunger.

Tribes that depend largely on hunting and very little on farming go through periods of hunger when game is scarce. If the Shawnees had been willing to farm as well as hunt, they might have eaten more regularly.

Possibly Daniel Boone suggested to Blackfish, during one of their long conversations around a fire in the wigwam, that the Shawnee men should help the women in the field, so the tribe would have more corn for the winter months. But if he did, we can be sure Blackfish rejected the idea. The Shawnees, like other hunting people, believed that farming was strictly women's work.

Daniel himself did not think that field work was humiliating, but he disliked it, so he was able to understand the Indians' point of view.

Shawnee men were not lazy. When the tribe was hungry, they went hunting even while blizzards were raging.

After one period of semistarvation, when the whole village went hungry for days, a party of braves marched in carrying several deer. The women then brewed a vile concoction for everyone to drink before eating. Daniel swallowed a little of the stuff and felt sick at his stomach. But the Indians explained that if he did not drink it, the fresh deer meat would make him sick. Soon his appetite returned, and he ate a big meal of venison without any ill effect.

Considering everything, Daniel enjoyed life as a Shawnee. He would have enjoyed it more if he had not been forced always to deceive the Indians in order to prepare for escape.

One day a party of Shawnee hunters arrived at Chillicothe and reported they had been ambushed by white men, led by Pequolly. The whites had killed and scalped several Shawnees.

Anger swept through the tribe. Again young warriors made speeches and said that every white man should be roasted. They wanted to organize a party to go immediately to attack Boonesborough.

Blackfish, a skillful politician, saw that something must be done. He said that the Shawnees were not yet ready to go to Kentucky. But he proposed that a war party be sent against the fort where Chief Cornstalk had been killed. The young men agreed. A war party was hastily assembled and sent off. A fortnight later this party returned and admitted defeat.

Blackfish knew that the march into Kentucky could

not be delayed much longer. He gave orders for a big war party to assemble. He still had hopes that Boone would persuade the Kentucky settlers to surrender. But he probably had his doubts, and he may have guessed that Daniel planned to escape.

Preparations were being made for the march on Kentucky. Warriors from other villages arrived, until more than five hundred men were gathered. In the council house the chiefs met daily and made plans. Women assembled a great store of provisions.

Soon a three-day fast would begin, during which the warriors would drink only a bitter concoction and would not sit down or even lean against anything from dawn until nightfall. After the fast, the long march would begin.

Daniel knew that he must try to escape now, no matter what chances he took.

One morning a party of warriors, followed by women leading pack horses, went to hunt a bear. Daniel went along, but did not have a rifle.

After they had gone a few miles, they scared up a large flock of turkeys. The warriors hurried after the turkeys.

This was the chance Boone had been waiting for. When shots rang out in the woods ahead, indicating that the warriors were busy with the turkeys, Boone cut the thongs and unloaded one of the horses.

Blackfish's wife was among the women. "My son," she cried, "what are you doing?"

"I am going to see my wife and children," he told her.

"You cannot go. Blackfish will be angry." She was almost in tears.

"I must."

"You will starve in the woods."

"I have some supplies hidden away," he told her. "I am very sorry to leave you and my father, Blackfish, and all my Shawnee brothers and sisters."

This was the truth. Daniel regretted leaving them, but he had no choice. He mounted and galloped away.

Boone plunged through the woods to the place where he had hidden his leather sack of dried meat and ammunition and his stockless rifle. Then he rode south all that day and night. When the horse was too tired to travel fast, he turned it loose and ran on foot.

Boone was then nearly forty-four years old, but few athletes in their prime could have kept up with him.

He had a slight advantage over the Shawnees pursuing him because he had taken the best horse. Also they would have to trail him, because they did not know which of the many routes he would take. To confuse this trail he sometimes waded in swift-flowing streams.

At the end of the second day he came to the Ohio River, which was swollen with the spring rains. Here he might have been trapped, for he could not swim, But he had a rare bit of luck. After ranging along the bank for some miles, he came upon an old canoe with a hole in its bottom. Working very fast, he plugged the hole and paddled across.

On the third day he passed Blue Licks, where he had been captured five months before.

He was now in fairly safe territory and was very hungry, having eaten his little supply of dried meat long before. He found a piece of wood which was about the right size and tied it to the breech of his stockless rifle. Then he killed a buffalo and had a feast. He cut out the tongue and carried it with him as a present for his eight-year-old son, Daniel Morgan Boone.

At the end of the fourth day he limped into Boonesborough. He had traveled 160 miles through the wilderness at the rate of forty miles a day.

It was a dismal homecoming. Of his own kin, only Jemima and her husband Flanders Callaway, and Squire Boone were there to greet him. His wife Rebecca had given him up for dead. She had taken the children back to North Carolina.

The settlers crowded around him. Men shook his hand and women cried. They all seemed tired and discouraged. Only Jemima was blooming and full of energy.

She waved the others away. "Pa has to rest," she said.

She led him to his cabin. It was bare and empty, but in a few minutes people came bringing furniture and utensils.

Daniel handed Jemima the buffalo tongue. "I brought this for the boy," he said, "but it'll likely spoil before I see him."

He sat down wearily, smiling at the excited people around him. There was a soft plop, and he looked down to see a cat in his lap. It was the Boone family cat and the special property of little Daniel Morgan Boone. It had been left behind when the family went east.

All of his life Daniel remembered the greeting of this cat.

The Shawnees Come

WHEN DANIEL BOONE ARRIVED, bringing word that
the Indians would soon attack, Boonesborough was
in no condition to defend itself.

Many of the settlers had fled east, leaving only a
dozen men, about a dozen boys big enough to aim a
rifle, and a few women and children. The gates of
the stockade were ready to collapse. Many logs in
the walls had rotted. Two-story blockhouses had been
built at only two of the four corners.

There were many stumps in the clearing around the
stockade, and weeds had grown up around them. A
warrior could creep up at night and hide behind one

of these stumps. From there he could fire at loopholes in the wall. There was one shallow well inside the stockade. It did not provide enough water for the people to drink, let alone for the cattle and horses that would be shut up there if the Indians attacked.

Daniel Boone had one of the settlers write a letter, which he signed, asking military authorities in Virginia to send reinforcements. Of course it would be months before such a force could arrive from Virginia. He also sent messages to the other Kentucky settlements, Logan's Station and Harrodsburg, pointing out that if Boonesborough fell, they would be next. He asked them to send every man they could spare.

Then he and the others set about repairing the gates, strengthening the walls, and building two more blockhouses. They started digging a new well, but quit digging before they struck water. Other things had to be done first.

About fifteen men and boys arrived from Logan's Station, and a few came from Harrodsburg, bringing the strength of the garrison to about thirty men and twenty boys. The total length of the stockade walls was about nine hundred feet. This meant that each man, with a boy or woman to load for him, would have to defend thirty feet of wall.

If three or four hundred Indians charged the walls from all sides at once, the whites could hope to kill only about twenty or thirty of them, and the others would swarm over the walls with tomahawks and knives.

If the Indians maintained a long siege, the whites would have to surrender for lack of water and food. Or if the Indians got even one cannon from the British, they could batter down the stockade walls in a few hours.

The people of Boonesborough considered these possibilities, and knew that their chances of living through the summer were not very great. But they were too busy to think much about death.

Daniel wanted very much to see his wife and family, but he could not leave Boonesborough at the time of its greatest danger. He was glad that Rebecca and the children were not there. At least he would not have to worry about them.

On July 17 someone heard a faint cry from across the river, and saw a man in rags wave his arms and fall at the water's edge. Boone and other riflemen stood on the bank while someone paddled over in a canoe to investigate. The ragged man proved to be William Hancock, one of the men who had been captured with Daniel at Blue Licks and adopted into the Shawnee tribe.

Hancock was hardly conscious when they carried him into the stockade, but a few hours later he was able to speak. He had slipped out of Chillicothe in the night and had spent nine days traveling.

He said the Shawnees had postponed the attack, waiting for the arrival of additional supplies from the British at Detroit. The British were sending four cannon. The Shawnee attack would come in a little over three weeks.

If the British kept their promise to provide cannon, and if the Indians were able to transport the cannon to Kentucky, Boonesborough was doomed — unless, of course, a large force of riflemen arrived from Virginia.

The stockade was now in good repair, and there was not much to do. Daniel grew restless. He could not sit still and wait for something to happen. He and twenty others saddled horses and rode north.

After they crossed the Ohio River, they proceeded very cautiously, keeping away from trails where they might meet war parties. They could not kill game for fear their shots would be heard, but each had brought along a sack of parched corn for food.

As they approached Chillicothe by a roundabout way, they discovered that the Indian army was already on the march. They followed it, spying whenever possible. Once, sneaking through the woods behind this army and far off to the side, they ran into a party of about thirty warriors. There was a sharp fight in which one Indian was killed. The others fled.

A few days later Daniel and his men became so hungry that they decided one shot would not make much difference. So they killed a buffalo and feasted.

They crossed the Ohio not far behind the army, and the next day, while the army was camped at Blue Licks, they slipped past it. On September fifth they rode into Boonesborough and announced that the Indians would arrive the following morning.

That night everybody worked furiously, storing up water and making other last-minute preparations.

The next morning Daniel instructed everyone to act calm and lazy if they went outside the stockade.

"Don't let them think we are worried," he said. "If you're out where they can see you, pretend you don't care where they are or what they do."

Most of the people stayed inside, fearing they would show their excitement if they went out. Every bucket, tub, barrel, or pot in the stockade was full of water, so that no one had to go to the spring.

About ten o'clock, Moses and Isaiah Boone, young sons of Squire, mounted their ponies and rode out to the river to let the ponies drink. Daniel, rifle in hand, strolled along beside them. It was a warm morning, and a blue haze hung over the trees of the surrounding forest.

Because of Daniel's calm manner, the boys were not at all worried. Perhaps they forgot that Indians were expected. As the ponies drank, Daniel saw a party of men some distance away. They were walking toward the fort and carrying two flags. The boys saw them also.

"The soldiers are coming from Virginia," they cried. "Let's ride to meet them."

"No," Daniel said, "they're not from Virginia. Let's go back. And don't hurry."

In about half an hour a lone figure approached, carrying a big white flag. From one of the corner blockhouses Daniel studied him.

"It's Pompey," he said, "the Negro Shawnee."

"Hello!" Pompey shouted. "Is Captain Boone there?"

No answer.

Pompey called again.

"Yes," Daniel called back.

"We've come to take you to Detroit," Pompey said. "I've got letters for you from the British commander."

"Bring them to the gate," Daniel replied.

Pompey hesitated.

"Sheltowee, come out." Daniel recognized the voice of Chief Blackfish, calling from the woods.

Boone conferred with others in the stockade.

"I'd better go and talk with them," he said. "There's just a chance that we can argue with them until the reinforcements arrive."

With some doubts, the others agreed.

Boone called to Blackfish and agreed to meet him at a certain tree stump. Then he walked out alone.

People in the stockade watched him walk out of rifle range. They saw the Indians spread down a blanket. They saw Daniel sit down.

"That's the last of Boone," one of the men said.

Shots End a Peace
Conference

Perhaps Daniel himself wondered if he would ever see the inside of the stockade again. But he seemed careless and friendly as he shook hands with Blackfish.

"Why did you run away from me?" Blackfish said.

"I wanted to see my wife and children. I could not stay longer."

Blackfish shook his head sadly. "You should have said so. I would have let you go any time."

Blackfish had never lied to Boone, and now he might well be telling the truth. Daniel was embarrassed.

Blackfish then handed Daniel a letter from the British commander at Detroit. The commander reminded him that he had promised to surrender and said that the young Indians were hard to control. The commander hoped Boone would be sensible and avoid a massacre.

Daniel realized that from the Indians' point of view, his own behavior had been dishonest. He did not enjoy telling Blackfish that the Boonesborough people would not surrender. Then he remembered that one of the Boonesborough men, William Bailey Smith, had been a major in the Virginia militia before the Revolution. Smith still had his scarlet uniform.

"I was gone so long from here," Daniel said, "that the Big Chief in Virginia sent out a new commander, and I am no longer captain here. The new captain is not willing to surrender, although I want him to."

"Go and get him," Blackfish said.

Boone went back to the stockade and soon fetched out Major Smith. In his scarlet coat and three-cornered hat with big ostrich plumes, Smith looked very much like a great commander.

Negotiations were resumed. Boone kept still, and Smith shook his head. Blackfish and the other chiefs

were patient. The argument went on for a long time.

After several hours, Boone and Smith returned to the stockade.

"I'm not going to take all the responsibility," Daniel told the settlers. "If we surrender, the Indians will probably take us to Detroit safely. If we don't, there will be a fight. If we lose, we will all be scalped. Make up your minds."

Squire Boone said he would never surrender, but would fight until he died. Most of the others said the same.

That afternoon Colonel Callaway, father of Betsey

and Fanny, went out with Boone and Major Smith for another conference. The Indians spread panther skins on the ground, within rifle range of the stockade.

Blackfish and other chiefs spoke for the Indians. A Frenchman named De Quindre represented the British commander at Detroit. Warriors stood around holding branches over the heads of the delegates.

Blackfish said he would like to be introduced to Mrs. Boone and the wives of the other white captains. Daniel hastily explained that white women were very much afraid of Indians and could not be persuaded to come outside the stockade. Then Blackfish presented several buffalo tongues as a present for the white women.

Major Smith, as "commander" of the stockade, pretended to oppose surrender because it would be so hard to transport women and children to Detroit.

"I brought forty horses," Blackfish said, "so they can ride in comfort."

After a long talk, the settlers said they would give their answer the next day.

When Boone, Smith, and Callaway went back to the stockade, Daniel explained the situation to the rest.

"Blackfish brought forty horses to carry the women and children," he said. "He must think we have hundreds of men."

The settlers decided to prove to Blackfish that he was right. Women and children put on men's hats or coonskin caps and poked their heads up over the stockade wall. Even shovels and brooms were dressed to look like riflemen.

Each of the thirty grown men in the garrison had several rifles in good working order, and many had shotguns. There were also some worn-out gun barrels which would never shoot again. So the Indians sometimes saw a couple of hundred gun barrels at once.

When Pompey appeared the next morning, with his flag of truce, Boone called to him that the whites had decided not to surrender.

Boone knew that the Indians would be very angry. He warned the settlers to get ready for trouble.

But hours passed, and no trouble came. Then the settlers had a surprise. Pompey returned with word that the Indians wanted peace. He suggested a conference for the next day. Daniel agreed.

"Tomorrow," he said to his men, "we must be careful. They have been honest with us so far, and they really thought we would surrender. But now they realize we have been tricking them to gain time. This offer is too good. They pretend to be more friendly than ever, and that is a danger sign."

Next morning several tables were carried to a large sycamore tree within rifle shot of the stockade. Daniel and Squire Boone, Major Smith, Colonel Callaway, Flanders Callaway, and three other whites sat down at the tables to represent Boonesborough. Blackfish brought seventeen chiefs with him, one to represent each of the Shawnee villages.

The Indian chiefs made long, dull speeches, but the Boonesborough men did not object. They wanted the conference to last as long as possible.

At noon the white men went into the stockade and brought out their best plates, knives and forks, and an elaborate meal. They regretted losing all this food, because their supplies were so short. But they wanted the Indians to think they had plenty of everything to withstand a siege.

The peace delegates feasted. Then Boone and the other Boonesborough men carried the plates, knives and forks, and all the leftovers back to the stockade.

In the afternoon the conference got down to drawing up an agreement. A clerk wrote down each clause when the delegates agreed upon it. The Ohio River was to be the boundary between the Shawnee and the white nations. The two peoples were to live in friendship always.

Daniel sometimes noticed Blackfish looking at him sadly, and he could guess what was going on in the old man's mind. Blackfish could not understand why Boone could possibly want to live in this dreary log fort and plant corn and milk cows when he could live the life of a Shawnee chief.

But it was plain that Blackfish had made up his mind. If Daniel would not keep the promise to his Shawnee brothers, then Blackfish could not show him any mercy.

Across the table, Boone and Blackfish watched each other suspiciously. The fact that they admired each other made no difference. They were enemies now, pretending to be friends while they planned war.

Late in the afternoon the agreement was completed, and the "peace treaty" was written. Blackfish said no treaty could be signed on the day it was written. Tomorrow morning they would meet again and go through the ceremony of peace.

Before leaving the stockade the next morning, Daniel placed his best riflemen along the wall overlooking the peace conference.

"If we wave our hats," he said, "you open fire. Don't bother to take aim, but fire into the lump. We'll get back the best we can. Leave the gate open a little so we can run in — but not very far open."

He and the seven other delegates stacked their rifles just inside the gate and walked out to the final meeting.

Blackfish and seventeen other Shawnees marched from the forest to the big sycamore tree near the stockade.

Boone had a feeling that something was going to happen, but he did not know just what. He noticed that the Indian delegation was made up mostly of young warriors instead of the old chiefs who had come the day before.

"You have different chiefs today," he said to Chief Blackfish.

"The same," Blackfish said.

The Indians carried no weapons except a peace pipe, but it was made in such a way that it was both a pipe and a tomahawk. Beneath the bowl was a blade. The pipe was lighted and passed around, but it was passed only to Indians.

Blackfish arose and explained that to conclude a treaty of peace, the Shawnees touched breasts together, to indicate the meeting of hearts. Since there were eighteen Indians and only eight white delegates, each white man would touch hearts with two Indians at the same time.

The whites lined up and the Indians faced them. Inside the stockade, riflemen leveled their long guns.

Boone realized that when the delegates put their hearts together, two strong warriors would have a hold on each white man. They were only a few steps from the bank of the river. Maybe the Indians intended to drag the white men over this bank.

No one knows exactly what either side intended to do at this moment. But we know what happened: A shot rang out. White and Indian delegates began wrestling. Guns blazed from the stockade.

The white men ran for the fort. A bullet knocked Squire Boone down. It could have come either from the stockade or from the nearby woods. Squire got to his feet and ran to the gate.

All but one of the delegates got through the gate; he was too late and had to flatten out behind a stump near the stockade wall and lie there.

A white man who wrote an account of this incident declares that the Indians planned to drag all the white delegates to the river, and that Blackfish himself gave the signal which started the fighting.

But if so, it seems that eighteen strong Indians could have held fast to at least one or two of the whites.

Probably the truth is that each side expected trouble at that moment. Rifles were cocked and aimed. Someone shouted or pulled a trigger. The fight was on.

As soon as they got inside the stockade, Daniel and the other delegates grabbed their rifles and began firing at clumps of bushes where Indians were hiding. Squire Boone had a bullet in his shoulder and was bleeding badly. He fired two shots and collapsed.

Daniel and another man carried him to his cabin. Daniel cut out the bullet and bandaged the wound. Squire was too weak to return to his place on the wall, but he asked them to leave an ax beside his bed. "When they break in," he said, "maybe I can get in a lick or two."

The last delegate was lying unhurt behind a stump near the stockade wall. Bullets from the nearby woods kicked dirt on him and slapped against the stump. All day he lay, not daring to move. When night came, someone opened the gate slightly and he crawled to safety.

Bullets and Flaming Arrows

The Indians had plenty of ammunition and they used it freely. Each of more than four hundred braves loaded and fired as fast as he could. The noise of their guns made a continuous roar all around the stockade, and the air became hazy with white smoke of burned powder. Bullets spatted against the logs and hissed through loopholes. The whites hardly dared to pop their heads above the wall.

The cattle had not been turned loose that morning. When the firing began, they stampeded around the enclosure, bawling with fright. Women and children screamed.

A rail fence extended from the stockade out to the edge of the timber where the Indians were hiding. The Indians scattered flax plants along the fence and set the flax afire. Flames crawled slowly along the fence toward the stockade.

The settlers hurriedly dug a tunnel under the wall of the stockade and up to the surface beneath the fence. They pulled fence rails into the tunnel, while bullets crashed just over their heads. Thus they made a gap in the fence so the flames could not get to the wall.

The firing continued all day and all night. At dawn it ceased. The settlers peered over the walls. From the woods came the clear note of a bugle. Indians did not use bugles, so the settlers knew that the Frenchman De Quindre was tooting.

Daniel heard shouts in Shawnee.

"Some chief is ordering the warriors to gather the pack horses," he said.

"They're leaving!" the settlers cried. "They're retreating. It's all over."

"Don't let them fool you," Boone said. "If they were really leaving, the main body would move off quietly. Only about fifty would stay to keep up a steady firing."

The bugle note came again, this time from farther away.

"They hope we will open the gate and come out to investigate. If we did, that would be the end of Boonesborough."

The settlers waited. The forest was quiet and peaceful. Birds chirped. But crows did not call calmly from the tree to signal safety.

In about an hour a war whoop sounded and hundreds of rifles spoke in a ragged volley.

Some Indians were firing from a nearby hill. By loading their rifles heavily and aiming at a high angle, the Shawnees could drop bullets into the stockade. Several settlers were hit and some badly wounded, but few died of their wounds.

On the third day a watcher in a blockhouse noticed that the water of the Kentucky River was muddy at the point where the bank came nearest to the stockade. In a little while the muddy streak extended far downstream. It was plain that the Indians were digging a tunnel from the riverbank toward the stockade. They were throwing the dirt into the water.

The Frenchman De Quindre was teaching the Indians European methods of siege warfare. If the Indians kept digging, they could go right under the stockade wall, and attack from underground.

Hurriedly the settlers constructed a watchtower of logs thick enough to stop bullets. They set it on the roof of one of the corner blockhouses. From the tower, riflemen could see dirt being thrown into the river, though they could not see the warriors who were throwing it.

Suddenly well-aimed bullets began killing livestock in the center of the enclosure. Boone climbed into the watchtower and saw that a warrior had established himself in the top of a tree some two hundred yards away.

Boone loaded his heaviest rifle and waited patiently. In a little while he saw the warrior's head among the leaves. He took careful aim and fired. The warrior pitched headlong to the ground.

It was the Negro Pompey. He had been born a slave of the whites, but had escaped and become an important member of the Shawnee tribe. Now he had died in battle, fighting for his adopted people.

Back in his cabin, Squire Boone had an idea. Lying in bed, he remembered that there was a big black gum log near his blacksmith shop. A black gum log cannot be split. To work it into firewood you have to saw it into short blocks and cut off slabs. Gum is one of the toughest and most contrary kinds of wood.

Squire sat up in bed with his grand idea. Why not make a cannon from this tough log?

About the fourth day of the siege he was able to get up and begin work with one hand. He and a helper heated iron and burned out the center of the log. Then they heated wagon tires and wrapped these metal bands around the log to make it stronger. Finally they mounted the heavy log on a swivel.

Squire put more than a pound of powder in his wooden cannon, plenty of wadding, about thirty one-ounce rifle balls, and perhaps a few scraps of iron which he found about the place.

One patch of bushes near the fort was always full of Indians. On a foggy morning, the settlers hoisted the cannon to the top of the stockade wall and aimed it at the bushes. All the men except Squire backed off to a safe distance.

Squire put the red-hot end of a rod to the touch-hole. There was a roar which shook the stockade and started the cattle stampeding again.

As the great cloud of white smoke lifted, the settlers saw a dozen Indians sprinting from the bushes toward the woods. The settlers sent up a great cheer.

Squire and his helper lowered the cannon and poured water into it, to put out the fire in the wood which the powder had started. When the cannon had dried a little, Squire loaded it again.

The others had confidence in the cannon now, and stood closer.

Squire touched it off. Another roar. The men standing nearest were knocked down. The gun had burst and was a tangled mass of kindling wood and wagon tires. Squire picked himself up and brushed the splinters out of his hair. Now at least it would not be much trouble to break the log up into firewood.

The siege had continued longer than anyone expected. Indians did not like siege operations. Sitting around behind stumps and firing at a log wall was not their idea of fighting. In other attacks the Indians had always retired after a couple of days.

The settlers were getting worried about the lengthening tunnel. But they were even more concerned over their dwindling water supply. They had saved a little water to use if the Indians set the stockade afire. But they knew they would soon have to drink it all just to keep alive.

Some of the settlers said that the Indians would not have the courage to rush through the tunnel, once it was completed.

Daniel told them they were wrong. Plenty of Indians would volunteer to push through, even though it meant almost certain death for the first ones.

It was Daniel's hope that the Indians would not finish their tunnel. Digging in the ground was considered disgraceful work for a warrior. He could guess how much trouble De Quindre was having in persuading the Indians to continue the degrading work.

But on the seventh day the settlers could hear the faint click of shovels as the Indians dug toward them. The braves had only a few more yards to dig.

It was a gloomy day, but no rain had fallen. A flaming arrow came from the bushes, arched high into the air, and fell on a cabin roof. A settler climbed up and beat out the flames with a broom while bullets whizzed around him.

A fire arrow struck another roof. Men from inside the cabin managed to break through the roof, knocking the shingles upward with their gun barrels. Many other arrows came, but most hit the ground inside the enclosure, where they did no damage.

Late in the day scores of these arrows arched into the stockades, and sometimes . three or four fires started at the same time Men, women, and boys beat out the flames.

Squire Boone was working furiously in his blacksmith shop, making a piston to fit in an old rifle barrel. When someone asked him what he was doing, he explained he was making a squirtgun. It seemed he had gone out of his mind, to be making a toy at such a time. But when he finished his squirtgun, he put out a blaze using only a pint of water.

As thick darkness settled, the attack increased in fury. Suddenly several warriors rushed toward the stockade carrying lighted torches. The defenders fired, but could not stop all of them. Some managed to fling their torches against the stockade wall.

One torch fell against a cabin door which faced outside the stockade. John Holder, Fanny Callaway's husband, pushed the blazing door open, ran outside the stockade, and threw a bucket of water on the flames. A dozen rifles cracked in the bushes. When John got back inside and bolted the door, he found several bullet holes through his clothing, but he had not been hit.

One Boonesborough man, William Patton, had been away from home on a long hunt and did not know of the Indian attack. As he neared home on this seventh night of the siege, he saw the stockade blazing, heard the rattle of rifle fire and whoops of Indians and screams of women.

He ran for Logan's Station and informed the settlers there that the Indians had captured Boonesborough and scalped the garrison.

He was mistaken. The Boonesborough people, with brooms and Squire's squirtgun, managed to put out every blaze before the walls were seriously damaged. Toward morning a drizzling rain began to fall. The Indians continued their fire attack, but cabin roofs burned more slowly. Finally, when the settlers were dropping from weariness, a heavy rain began to fall.

They caught rainwater in buckets and drank their fill. Then the women and children huddled in those cabins which still had roofs and went to sleep. Men dozed at their posts.

All the next day the rain came in torrents. Rifles cracked from the woods, whenever a man looked over the stockade wall. The Indians were still there.

When night came the rain slackened, but the sky did not clear. Indians might be creeping up ready to leap over the walls. The men were now so tired that they fell asleep standing up.

At dawn everyone was awakened by a shout. A man in the watchtower was pointing toward the river.

"Look what happened!" he called.

Men and women leaped up, ran to the wall, and looked over.

A deep pit extended from the riverbank almost to the wall. Because of the heavy rain, the roof of the tunnel had fallen in.

"That's the end," Daniel said. "They won't try any more."

He was right. At sunup, he and others went out and looked around. The Indians were gone.

Around each loophole in the stockade walls there was a thick crust of lead, where bullets had lodged in the wood and flattened out, one on top of the other. That day the settlers gathered a hundred and twenty-five pounds of lead from the walls and the nearby ground.

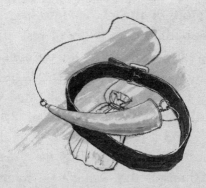

A Thief in the Night

On the first day after the siege was lifted, the people of Boonesborough had plenty of energy. They were so glad to be alive that they thought little of their ruined crops or their other losses.

But there is nothing like a day of rest to bring out deep-seated weariness. Soon they were sunk in gloom. Several of their best cows had been killed inside the stockade. The Indians had killed all game within ten miles. The settlers had plenty of lead but little powder.

People began to hate each other. Women scolded and men snarled over trifles. To his great disgust, Daniel found himself the center of a lively and unpleasant controversy.

His old friend Colonel Callaway suddenly turned on him and said that he, Daniel Boone, was the cause of all their troubles.

Callaway declared that Daniel had betrayed the men at the salt camp and helped the Shawnees capture them.

Daniel pointed out that the Indians themselves had found the camp and would have killed all the men if Daniel hadn't talked them out of it.

"You joined the Shawnee tribe and plotted with them to destroy this settlement," Callaway roared.

"Why did I escape from them and come back here?" Daniel asked.

"That was part of the scheme —"

"Why did I stay here and help you fight them off, when I wanted to go back to North Carolina and see my family? Why did I risk my scalp —"

"You planned to turn us all over to the British —"

Flanders Callaway sided with Daniel, even though the colonel was his uncle. So did most of the other Boonesborough people. But the colonel continued to roar. Daniel insisted on a public hearing.

Most of the men at the three Kentucky settlements belonged to the Kentucky militia. Daniel was a captain in that organization. He said that this argument was a militia matter. He demanded a trial before a regular court-martial.

Officers of the militia were called in from Logan's Station and Harrodsburg. A trial was held. Colonel Callaway repeated his charges and demanded that Boone's commission be taken from him.

Daniel told his story. The court-martial immediately declared he was not guilty. Soon after that he was promoted from captain to major.

About the time this argument was settled, reinforcements arrived from Virginia. Boonesborough was safe at last. Daniel Boone saddled a horse and went down the Wilderness Road toward North Carolina. He was taking a vacation from the hard job of fighting Indians and conquering the wilderness.

No one knows exactly what he did during the following twelve months. He found Rebecca and the children safe and well, living in a small cabin on a farm belonging to her relatives. Certainly Daniel had some fascinating tales to tell, when the family and neighbors gathered around the fireplace on a long winter evening.

Meanwhile important events were happening west of the mountains. A small army of Virginians under George Rogers Clark pushed into the Northwest, as the country north of Kentucky was then called, and captured three British forts. Without these forts the British found it much more difficult to stir up the Indians.

In the spring of 1779, while Daniel was in North Carolina, about two hundred men from the Kentucky settlements attacked Chillicothe.

The Indians were not expecting this attack. Blackfish with a party of warriors had just left town. Only twenty-five warriors and fifteen boys were left to defend it. Women and children huddled in the council house while the warriors and boys tried to defend the village. A messenger got through the lines and told Blackfish what was happening.

Blackfish and his party returned to Chillicothe and charged through the white lines. Blackfish was badly wounded in the leg. Some of the Indians suggested that they surrender, in the hope that the white men would have some magic medicine which would save Blackfish's life. But the old chief refused to surrender. After a few hours of fighting, the whites withdrew.

Blackfish died several weeks later.

In the fall of 1779, Daniel Boone, two of his younger brothers, and a dozen other farmers, each with a large family, started for Kentucky. One of these farmers was named Abraham Lincoln. His grandson, born thirty years later in Kentucky, became the sixteenth President of the United States.

Some of Daniel's neighbors who did not go on the trip took up a collection and bought Daniel two cannons, called "swivel guns."

Because the trail had been widened, it was now possible to make the trip in wagons. Each family had one or more covered wagons. A man who saw the wagon train depart said it was a half-mile long and looked more like an army than a party of settlers.

Before they had gone far, some of the horses died. Daniel discovered that in order to ford the Cumberland River he would have to throw away either some provisions or the cannons. He knew they would need these big guns when the Indians attacked. But he was more afraid of hunger during the coming winter than he was of Indians. He left the guns beside the river, hoping someday to send a party back to get them. They were made of bronze and would not rust. But he never sent for them. There was always too much to do in Kentucky.

The wagon train did not stop at Boonesborough, probably because Daniel did not want to live too near his one-time friend, Colonel Callaway. Instead, Daniel started a new settlement, called Boone's Station, a few miles north.

Soon other wagon trains crawled past Boone's Station, and several settlements were established between the Licking and Kentucky rivers, north of Boone's Station. Kentucky was booming again.

For a few months at least, the new settlers did not have to fear Indian attacks. George Rogers Clark and his Virginians had built a fort at the falls of the Ohio, northwest of the Kentucky settlements. They were prepared to move against any large Indian army that crossed the Ohio.

But the settlers that winter had two other enemies as dangerous as Indians: cold and hunger. Winter came early. Layers of ice covered the trees and grass. Snow piled up in the hollows so that the wagons could not travel. Cattle and hogs froze to death.

Food supplies that the newcomers had brought from the East in their covered wagons were soon eaten up. The price of corn went to sixty dollars a bushel. The people at Boone's Station listened to the wind howling outside their cabins and wondered if they would be alive when spring came.

Perhaps many of the newcomers, as they huddled in their cabins, half starved and blue with cold, wished they had never left their comfortable homes in North Carolina. But before anyone actually starved, honks sounded from the gray sky, and fat geese and ducks settled on pools in the woods. Men loaded their guns and hid in the canebrakes. Soon everyone was eating roast goose and duck. Kentucky was once again a wonderful place.

But now the settlers had another problem to solve: Could they prove that they owned their own land? To stake a true claim to a piece of land, they had to pay a certain sum of money to the Virginia government. The settlers had the money. The problem was how to send it to Virginia.

Daniel was the man they trusted most, and they insisted that he carry their money to Virginia. It was not the sort of job he liked, but he had no choice. With between forty and fifty thousand dollars in his saddlebag, he started east with one companion.

Daniel Boone could outwit honest Indians in the woods, but he was no match for dishonest whites. He and his companion got safely through the mountains, and stopped at an inn in James City, Virginia. Here they ate a big meal, went to their room, and carefully locked the door. Daniel put the saddlebag beside the bed.

The next morning he awoke, dizzy and bewildered. Evidently he and his companion had been drugged.

His papers were scattered about the room. The door was open. The saddlebag and some of his clothes were missing.

He shook his companion awake and the two, half dressed, began a search. They found the saddlebag at the foot of the stairs, empty. The missing garments had been thrown out the window into the garden.

They searched the inn from cellar to attic and found a little of the paper money in some jugs in the cellar.

Daniel believed that the landlord had planned the robbery. But he could prove nothing.

He returned sorrowfully to Kentucky. Every cent of his own money had been in the saddlebag, too. So he could not pay back the money he had lost.

Few of the settlers blamed him. Some told him to forget about the money. In later years he was able to pay the others in land for the money which had been stolen from him.

Rifle Shots
in the Woods

Daniel Boone and Colonel Callaway would probably have patched up their differences and become friends again if they had had a chance. Daniel was not one to hold a grudge. Callaway, although sometimes angry and blustering, was honest and well-meaning. Undoubtedly, Daniel's daughter, Jemima Callaway, would have brought Daniel and the Colonel together. But she never had the opportunity.

In March, 1780, about the time that Daniel was being robbed in Virginia, Colonel Callaway and another man were killed and scalped by the Indians about a mile and a half from Boonesborough. The same day a third man was killed in the nearby woods. Within a week Squire Boone and several other men were wounded. It was plain that British agents were again stirring up the Indians.

In June, several hundred Indians and a few British soldiers raided Kentucky. They brought two cannons with them. With these big guns they easily demolished two new stockades near Blue Licks, north of Boone's Station. The Indians killed some of the captives taken on this raid, but permitted the British to take most of them to Detroit.

In retaliation, George Rogers Clark and his soldiers from Virginia left their fort at the Falls of the Ohio. They collected a force of Kentucky riflemen and invaded the Shawnee country. Daniel Boone commanded a detachment from Boone's Station and Boonesborough on this raid. The Virginians and Kentuckians burned Chillicothe and other Indian towns. Some of Clark's soldiers got out of hand and killed several captives, including a woman.

The Kentuckians hoped that their raid would teach the Indians to keep out of Kentucky, but they were wrong.

One night, on a hunting trip, Daniel and twenty-five

of his men camped in the woods south of the Kentucky River. While the others were relaxing after supper, Daniel heard something which made him uneasy. Perhaps a night bird somewhere off in the woods called out in surprise. Or perhaps there was silence where there should have been noise. Daniel did not explain, but slipped away from the group.

Soon he was back. "They're all around us," he said. "Roll up some blankets so they will look like men asleep."

He gathered an armful of twigs and put them on the fire in such a way that they would smolder for a while and then blaze up briefly. "Before this wood catches fire," he said, "we'll crawl off into the bushes."

The men followed his instructions. When the fire blazed up, Indians hidden a few hundred yards away saw what looked like men sleeping peacefully. Then the fire died down. Hours passed and nothing happened. Probably some of the men wondered if Daniel's imagination had gotten the better of him.

With the first light of dawn, rifles cracked and bullets went through the blanket rolls. There was a war whoop. Indians charged toward the campsite. The whites opened fire. The Indians fell on their faces and crawled away, dragging their wounded with them.

On another occasion Daniel was hunting alone near Blue Licks. Beside a little stream called Slate Creek he saw signs of Indians.

He got out of sight and cautiously followed the trail for several miles. Approaching a small spring, he listened and watched for a while. Then he crept forward and took a drink. A shot sounded nearby, and a bullet knocked the bark from a tree trunk just above his head. He leaped up, ran to a thicket, and from there worked his way to a canebrake beside the creek. Here he hid and waited.

There was a stir in the bushes on the hillside and two brown heads appeared. If Daniel shot one of them, the other would shoot before he could reload. If he ran, they would chase him and could probably keep between him and the nearest white settlement. The canebrake was small.

He knew they were good woodsmen because they had already outwitted him, hiding so well that he came within shooting range without seeing them. His only advantage lay in marksmanship. He could save his scalp only by luck and a careful shot.

As they crept toward him, he drew a bead on the head of the first one and waited. The second raised himself to have a look. Daniel pulled the trigger. His bullet went through the head of the first and struck the second in the shoulder, knocking him down. The second dropped his gun and ran.

In October, 1780, Daniel and his younger brother Edward went on horseback to Blue Licks to make salt. On their return journey, they halted beneath a hickory tree to crack nuts and let their horses graze.

Daniel saw a bear almost out of shooting range. Game was scarce and the settlement needed meat, so Daniel fired. The bear lumbered off, but Daniel knew it was wounded and would soon drop dead. He ran after it, neglecting to reload. Just as he found the carcass, he heard shots behind him, then the baying of a hound. He knew that Edward was either dead or a prisoner, and nothing could be done for him.

Daniel started reloading just as the hound came in sight. Knowing that the Indians would be close behind the dog, he sprinted for a nearby canebrake. His ramrod slipped out of his hand as he ran, and he could not stop to pick it up.

He reached the canebrake before the Indians caught sight of him, but he knew he could not hide if the dog kept on his trail.

Daniel broke off a slender stalk of cane to use as a ramrod and finished reloading. When the dog came in sight again he shot it.

Daniel went back to the settlement, and the next day led a party to the place. They found Edward's body and trailed the Indians as far as the Ohio. On the way back they stopped to hunt, for in Kentucky in those days little time could be spared to mourn the dead. The living must have food.

Kentucky was then a part of Virginia, and the settlers elected Daniel as one of their representatives in the Virginia State Assembly. In April of the following year, 1781, he was attending a session of the

Assembly at Charlottesville, Virginia, when a force of two hundred and fifty British soldiers galloped into town.

The legislators ran into the woods and hid, except Daniel and a few others who remained to load some official papers in a wagon. After this chore was done, Daniel and a man named Jouett mounted their horses and started away calmly. Parties of soldiers dashed past them, looking for members of the Assembly.

Daniel was dressed frontier-style, in a buckskin hunting shirt, trousers, and leggings. He did not look at all like a member of the Assembly or a high officer in the Kentucky militia.

But when he and Jouett walked their horses out of town, a squad galloped up to them and began asking questions.

Daniel said they were on their way home. He asked them how the war was going, in a tone which indicated he did not care how it was going.

The soldiers rode along beside them, trying to make up their minds about these country characters. Daniel bored them with some talk about his troubles out on the farm. The sergeant in command of the squad began to lose interest.

They came to a crossroad and Jouett said to Daniel, "Well, Colonel, this is our road."

"Colonel!" shouted the sergeant.

The soldiers took the two men back to town and locked them up.

But Daniel was not easy to keep. No one knows how or when he escaped from the British, but in August he was back in Kentucky. In September he visited his boyhood home in Pennsylvania, where some of his relatives still lived. From November until January, 1782, he again served as a member of the Virginia Assembly.

The Revolutionary War was now over, although peace had not been declared. But the British still hoped to keep the land west of the mountains.

For Kentucky, the year 1782 would be "the year of blood."

The Battle of Blue Licks

THE BRITISH AT DETROIT continued to stir up trouble among Shawnees. Raids and massacres continued along the Pennsylvania and Virginia frontiers. One side was as bloodthirsty as the other.

Many Indians still lived east of the mountains. They had adopted "the white man's way," and had no quarrel with anybody. A mob of white men attacked one village of unarmed Indian farmers and murdered ninety-six men, women, and children.

The British told the Shawnees of this massacre and warned them that the same thing would happen to them if they ever made peace with the Long Knives.

Soon after that, in June, 1782, about five hundred Pennsylvanians and Virginians invaded Shawnee territory. The Shawnees defeated them in a battle on the Sandusky River in Ohio, and burned their commander at the stake.

The fierce Wyandot Indians lived west of Kentucky. They had always been enemies of the Shawnees. But when the Wyandots heard that the whites had killed unresisting Indians in the east, they made peace with the Shawnees and sent war parties into Kentucky.

One morning early in August, the settlers at a new stockade, called Bryan's Station, discovered that their hundred-acre cornfield was full of Indians.

Plainly the Indians were waiting for the whites to open the gates and go out to work. The whites kept the gates closed. There was no well inside the stockade and the water buckets were empty. If flaming arrows set the cabins afire, they could not fight the flames. The weather was hot. The whites would soon suffer from thirst.

But the women had an idea. "Let us go out to the spring, carrying buckets as we always do, and laughing and talking. The Indians will be sure that we do not know they are there. They will wait for you men to come out before they begin shooting."

At first the men objected. It was too dangerous, they said.

But the women argued. If they didn't get water, the stockade would burn down and they would all be scalped anyway.

The women opened the gate slightly and went out with their buckets, talking in lively fashion. In groups of three or four they walked to the spring, a short distance from the stockade, and filled their buckets. Some made a second trip.

Two men mounted horses and rode out of the gate at a walk. They talked lazily to each other, pretending they were going out to work and were in no hurry.

When all the women had returned with their buckets and the two horsemen were out of sight, the settlers pulled the gate shut.

The Indians realized at last that the whites knew they were there. About a dozen Indians walked toward the back of the stockade, in plain sight of the settlers. They hoped that most of the white men would come out of the back gate and chase them, thus leaving the front of the stockade undefended.

But the whites knew this trick also. Twenty-five of their best riflemen, each with two or three loaded rifles, remained on the front side. Only ten or twelve men ran out the back gate to pretend to chase the Indians. They fired rifles and shouted, making as much noise as they could.

A hundred or more Indians charged the front. The

riflemen there had a good target. Dozens of Indians fell, and the others ran back to shelter.

All day long the Indians continued to fire on the stockade. Fire arrows ignited some cabin roofs, but the settlers put out the flames before much damage was done. One flaming arrow landed in the cradle of a baby named Richard Mentor Johnson, but the baby was unhurt. He grew up to become the ninth Vice-President of the United States.

Meanwhile the two horsemen, who rode out so lazily that morning, had galloped to a nearby settlement. In the afternoon, a party of sixteen horsemen and thirty riflemen came to relieve the besieged stockade. The horsemen charged straight through the Indian lines and reached the stockade without any losses. The thirty men on foot got into the cornfield and fought a battle, but had to retire after two of them were killed.

The Indians knew that more whites would soon arrive, so they slipped away and marched north toward Blue Licks.

Early the next morning Daniel Boone arrived with a detachment of men from Boonesborough and Boone's Station.

Dead cattle, sheep, and hogs lay bloating in the sun. All buildings outside the stockade had been burned. A field of hemp was ruined. Potato vines had been pulled up. Every stalk in the big cornfield had been broken or stripped of its leaves. The Indians had worked hard to destroy the property of the whites.

This was war.

Soon detachments from two other settlements arrived. A little less than two hundred fighting men were now present. Most of them wanted to follow the Indians immediately, although the Indians supposedly outnumbered them.

An officer in one detachment, Major Hugh McGary, pointed out that four or five hundred men would arrive next day from the settlements farther south. He suggested that they wait for reinforcements.

Colonel John Todd, commander of that detachment, ridiculed McGary. He hinted that McGary was afraid. Todd said if they waited another day the Indians would get safely across the Ohio.

The men were in a fighting mood, and almost all of them agreed with Todd. At noon they took up the trail.

Daniel was worried. The men were too angry to have good judgment. Like all frontier fighters, they lacked discipline. They obeyed a command if they felt like it. Daniel knew how dangerous it was for a crowd — they could not be called an army — of angry whites to engage a band of well-disciplined Indians.

Daniel was also worried about his son Israel, now twenty-three years old. Israel had insisted on coming along, although he had a fever. He had a strong constitution, but fever can strike down the strongest man.

Daniel studied the trail the Indians had left and did not like what he saw. The Indians were moving slowly. They were blazing the trail as they went, so the Kentuckians could follow easily.

The men marched all afternoon and most of the night. Next morning they came to the Licking River at Blue Licks. Here the river made a horseshoe bend around a big bare hill.

Colonel Todd asked Daniel's opinion. Daniel pointed to the hill across the river. "Just behind the bare hill," he said, "are two ravines. I'm sure the Indians are hiding there. They hope we will cross here and march up the hill. Then they will have us trapped, with the river on three sides. We'd better wait for reinforcements."

Major McGary had been accused of cowardice for making the same suggestions the day before. There was an angry murmur among the men. They made it plain that they were not going to wait.

"If you're bound to fight now," Boone said, "most of us should go upstream to Elk Creek, where there's a good ford. We can cross there, to get in position to attack from the flank. Then a few should cross here, making a lot of noise. We'll attack from the side when they're looking this way."

Major McGary had been in a sulk ever since he had been accused of cowardice. He wanted to prove he was no coward. He made a sneering remark about people who were afraid of Indians.

"What did we come here for?" McGary yelled at the men.

"To fight Indians!" they answered.

"Then let's fight 'em!" He slapped his horse with the reins and rode into the river.

Most of the men followed in a disorderly crowd. Boone, Todd, and the leader of the third detachment, Stephen Trigg, were left alone.

"We've got to go with them and get them into some kind of order," Daniel said.

The three commanders forded the river and formed their men into thin battle lines. Trigg took the right, Todd the center, and Boone the left. All the men dismounted and left their horses standing, reins down, near the river, except McGary and about twenty-five others who were in a hurry to fight.

They walked to the top of the hill and started down the other side toward the ravines. McGary whooped. He and the other mounted men charged toward the thicket.

The bushes spurted flame and white smoke, and the ground shook with the roar of hundreds of rifles. Men and horses went down in a tangled mass as the smoke cloud rolled over them.

Boone and his men charged toward the ravine ahead of them, crouching as they ran. The Indians at this end of the line fired too soon, and only a few of Boone's men were hit. The others leaped into the ravine with their rifles still loaded. A desperate game of hide-and-seek began.

Many of the Indians ran for their lives. Others tried

to remain hidden as they reloaded. Daniel that day was carrying, not his usual rifle, but a fowling piece — a large shotgun — loaded with three or four balls and a dozen buckshot.

He knew that an Indian was hiding somewhere near him. His rule was never look for an Indian — because you can't see him. Look for his gun, which he can't hide.

Daniel watched until he saw the long rifle barrel being cautiously leveled in his direction.

"You be there!" he shouted and pulled the trigger of his fowling piece.

Knowing that at least some of his buckshot had found its mark, he stood up cautiously to see if any other Indians remained in the ravine. All was clear. His men had won their part of the battle.

Behind him he heard a shout. McGary rode up.

"Colonel Boone," he yelled. "Retreat. They broke our lines."

Boone climbed out of the ravine and looked around. The battle had been going on only about five minutes. Just a few of Todd's and Trigg's men were still alive, and they were racing toward the river.

Boone gathered his men and began a retreat. A force of Indians charged them, but were stopped by a volley. A riderless horse trotted past. Daniel caught the horse and ordered his sick son, Israel, to mount and ride for the river.

"I won't leave you," Israel said. "I'm all right."

Daniel reloaded his gun.

A shot from a nearby thicket and Israel fell. Daniel picked him up. An Indian with a tomahawk ran toward them. Daniel dropped Israel and shot the Indian. When he picked Israel up again, he saw that his son was dead.

He carried the body toward the river, but knew he could not get across with it. There was a cave nearby where he had once camped. He hid the body there. Then he caught a horse and rode after his men. He managed to get most of them safely across the river.

A few men from the other detachments also got across, including McGary, who was largely responsible for the defeat. The Indians did not attempt to follow them far on their retreat.

During the rest of his long life, Daniel Boone blamed himself for the defeat at Blue Licks. He felt he should have thought of some way to make the men listen to him.

No one else blamed him. "This wouldn't have happened if we had done what Colonel Boone told us to do," they said.

The New Start

THE BATTLE OF BLUE LICKS was the last pitched battle of the Revolution. The thirteen colonies had won their independence, and the settlers in Kentucky had won the fight for the new land, although they did not know it for many months.

The following summer, 1783, a man rode into Boone's Station with a big piece of paper stuck in his cap. On the paper was written the word "Peace." He brought news that a peace treaty had been signed between Britain and the American states.

Small bands of Indians came to Kentucky that summer, ambushed and scalped settlers, destroyed crops and took horses. But to Daniel Boone and other old Indian fighters, such small raids seemed tame.

Daniel and Rebecca built a cabin three miles west of the stockade and settled there for what they hoped would be a quiet life of farming. Daniel planted a patch of tobacco and built a shed for drying the stalks. Tobacco was a good cash crop.

The shed was tall and had crossbeams at three levels, one above the other. Daniel's first crop filled the shed from top to bottom. One day after the stalks were dry and about ready to take to market, he climbed up to inspect the stalks on the upper level. He was careful not to shake them. A dry stalk of tobacco is covered with a fine dust. If you get this dust in your eyes, you are blinded for a while; and if you breathe it, you start sneezing and coughing.

Daniel was standing on a beam, when he heard a noise and looked down to see several Shawnee warriors in the shed, with their rifles pointed at him.

"Boone," they said, "this time we got you. You come with us to Chillicothe."

Daniel was unarmed. If he did not come down, they could shoot him, scalp him, and escape without difficulty. If he surrendered, they could take him and Rebecca and the children north, and the neighbors would probably never know what happened to the Boone family.

Daniel said he would climb down in a minute, but first he wanted to pick out his best stalk of tobacco to give his Shawnee friends.

He lifted a stalk carefully from its peg. The Indians were looking up at him, eyes and mouths open.

He held his breath, squinted his eyes almost shut

and shook the dusty stalk in the upturned faces. He kicked a beam with all his strength, and the force of his kick shook the whole shed. A cloud of brown dust filled the air.

Daniel leaped to the floor of the shed and ran out the door. The Indians yelled, coughed, sneezed, wept, and felt their way out of the shed. They trotted toward the woods, for they knew that Daniel was safe in his cabin and would soon have a big fowling piece, loaded with buckshot, aimed at them.

But except for these minutes of excitement, farm life was very dull. Daniel and Rebecca moved to a newly built town on the Ohio River. Daniel became a trader, surveyor, and real-estate dealer. He was elected a member of the legislature. But business and politics were as dull as farming.

Sometimes he was rich. Usually he was poor. Men cheated him in land deals. He became hopelessly entangled in lawsuits. He forgot to file claims to land. He was no match for shrewd land speculators who flocked into Kentucky.

For years Daniel tried to make himself over into a businessman and politician, but it was no use. He and Rebecca moved from place to place, but they were never happy except when they went on camping trips far from the settlements.

But Daniel could not afford to go on camping trips very often. A man could no longer make a living by hunting alone.

In 1795, Daniel's youngest son, Daniel Morgan Boone, went on a long hunting and exploring trip across the Mississippi River, into the land then owned by Spain. He returned with glowing accounts. Daniel began to make new plans.

In 1799, when he was nearly sixty-five, Daniel cut down a large tulip poplar tree on the bank of a stream which flows into the Ohio. From the trunk he made a dugout canoe sixty feet long, capable of carrying five tons.

Daniel's brother Squire, and Daniel's two sons, Daniel Morgan and Nathan, also made big canoes. Neighbors heard that the Boones were going West, and several other families made boats.

In September the flotilla started. Rebecca, her daughter Jemima Callaway, and most of the others went in the boats. Daniel and Flanders Callaway drove a herd of livestock along the bank. They were going West to begin life anew, where the hunting was still good.

Elbow Room

THE NEXT TWENTY YEARS were to Daniel the most satisfactory years of his life. Few men have lived so vigorously and fully after the age of sixty-five.

Often he was irritated, disappointed. Sometimes people interfered in his affairs. He had one very great loss. But most of the time he did exactly as he pleased.

Even the strenuous trip to Missouri was pleasant. The word spread through all Kentucky that the Boones were pushing off to a new wilderness. In covered wagons, on horseback, or in canoes along the streams, old friends came north to the Ohio River to say good-bye. Daniel and Rebecca saw many of their old friends and met hundreds of new friends too — people who had heard of Daniel Boone for years and now had a chance actually to see him!

Daniel's first big annoyance came at St. Louis. Spain then owned the great expanse of land called Louisiana, which spread like a large fan from the mouth of the Mississippi northward to the Canadian border. Spanish officials wanted people to settle in this territory. They knew that wherever Daniel Boone went, others would follow. So the Spanish governor at St. Louis organized a parade and a big reception in Daniel's honor.

Daniel did not enjoy parades and receptions in his own or anybody else's honor. He was embarrassed when people crowded around and cheered. But he suffered through the ordeal. He wanted to establish good relations with the Spanish authorities.

The governor told Daniel to select ten thousand or so acres for himself anywhere north of the Missouri River, and to parcel out smaller farms to each of the men who came with him. Daniel thanked the governor. As soon as all the fancy doings were over he pushed on into the wilds.

About sixty miles west of the confluence of the Missouri and Mississippi rivers, Daniel founded a settlement called Missouriton. There was plenty of land for everybody. Daniel and each of the men who came with him staked out a farm and built a cabin. Most of them cleared a patch of land for farming But Daniel had no time to clear land. The hunting was too good.

At first he hunted close to the settlement. But in the fall of 1801 he went on a long hunt, taking with him a Negro boy as campkeeper. He caught only fifty beaver, probably because he spent most of his time exploring.

The next fall he and the boy went out again and ran into trouble. They had just established a comfortable camp, and Daniel had taken a few pelts, when a party of Indians charged into camp and grabbed up everything worth grabbing. They even pulled Daniel's coat off his back.

But Daniel still knew how to handle people, including Indians. He laughed at them, taunted them, and threatened them in his usual reckless, friendly manner. They decided he must have some powerful magic about him, or he would be more afraid of them. They gave back most of his stuff and left him in peace.

During summer seasons when he was not hunting, Daniel acted as judge and lawmaker for the settlement. He held court under a big tree near his cabin. Here he settled land disputes and decided how wrongdoers should be punished. He made up his laws and rules as he went along, and the people were satisfied. His law was good enough for them.

In 1803 the United States purchased Louisiana, and in March of the following year American officials took possession. Daniel's land troubles began again.

Under Spanish law, a man was supposed to cultivate a part of the land he claimed. American officials said Daniel did not own any land because he had not done any cultivating. Daniel was disgusted. He wrote dignified letters to some of his influential friends in the East, asking them to take the matter up in Congress. Then he went hunting again.

During the War of 1812 a small band of Indians attacked one of the outlying cabins of the Missouriton settlement, wounding a man and three children. Daniel dressed their wounds with the skill he had acquired years before in Kentucky. A settler who watched him at this task wrote, "The old pioneer was quiet and unexcited as usual, but his lips were compressed and a fire gleamed in his eyes."

Daniel suffered the greatest loss of his life when Rebecca died in 1813. He selected a site for her grave on top of a mound overlooking the Missouri River. He felt he would soon join her there, and he always liked the top of a hill where the view was good.

About a year later he learned that the Congress of the United States had granted him a thousand acres of land in recognition of his "many eminent services" in exploring and settling the western country. At last he had a clear and undisputed title to a piece of land. He sold the land, paid his debts, and went hunting.

No one knows how far Daniel explored before and after the War of 1812. He may have gone as far as what is now Yellowstone Park. When he was eighty-two years old, he walked into Fort Osage, near where Kansas City now stands. An officer there wrote:

"We have been honored by a visit from Colonel Boone, the first settler of Kentucky; he lately spent two weeks with us. . . . The colonel cannot live without being in the woods. He goes a-hunting twice a year to the remotest wilderness he can reach."

During one of these hunts, a band of Osage Indians rode up to his camp and demanded that he give them his pelts. But Daniel was not in a mood to give away anything. He cocked his long rifle and aimed it at the leader of the band.

The Indians were amazed, not knowing they were dealing with the most experienced Indian fighter in the world. They had not expected trouble from an old man with long white hair. They looked at the rifle and at the old man's face. They rode away.

On another of these trips, when he was far from home, Daniel became ill. This was a new experience for him, and he decided his time had come. He gave careful instructions to his boy campkeeper.

"When I die," he said, "wash me and wrap me in the cleanest blanket. Dig a hole on top of that hill and bury me there, and put poles over the grave so the wolves can't dig down. Then go back to the settlement and tell my kin. They'll want to dig me up and bury me beside my wife."

But a few days later Daniel felt better, got up, and picked up his rifle.

If for any reason Daniel did not feel up to a long hunt, he stayed at home and played with his grandchildren. In 1817, when he was eighty-three, he went back to Kentucky to visit old friends. Kentuckians were very proud of him by this time. They held a big reception in his honor. But Daniel slipped away from the gathering as soon as he could.

"I dislike to be in a crowd where I have to receive so much attention." he said.

Tired of fame, he went back to Missouri to play

with the children and plan another hunt.

On September 26, 1820, when he was nearly eighty-six years old, Daniel died peacefully in his sleep at the home of his son Nathan. They buried him next to Rebecca on the high mound.